Questions

The Question of Religion

Questions

A series of explorations by
William Corlett and John Moore

THE QUESTION OF RELIGION
THE CHRIST STORY
THE HINDU SOUND

In preparation

THE JUDAIC LAW
THE BUDDHA WAY
THE ISLAMIC SPACE

WILLIAM CORLETT
&
JOHN MOORE

The Question of Religion

HAMISH HAMILTON

LONDON

First published in Great Britain 1978
by Hamish Hamilton Ltd,
90 Great Russell Street, London WC1B 3PT

ISBN 0 241 89770 X

Printed in Great Britain
by Ebenezer Baylis and Son Ltd,
The Trinity Press, Worcester and London

This book is one of a series.

The titles are *The Question of Religion*, *The Christ Story*, *The Hindu Sound*, *The Judaic Law*, *The Buddha Way* and *The Islamic Space*. The books were written in the order as listed, but this in no way implies any suggested precedence of one religion over another nor any preference on the part of the authors. Each book may be read in its own right, rather as each note of an octave may sound alone.

However, for an octave to be complete, it depends on the developing frequency and character of each note. In the same way, it has been the experience of the authors, approaching this series as one work, to find a similar development as they progressed from one book to another.

One

There is a story—this is a way of telling it.

Once upon a time, when the world was fresh and green and young, Man lived and worked in the valley beside the holy mountain.

He had been told that he had been created immortal, that the gods held his Spirit for him on the holy mountain and that, in time, it would be given to him and he would take his place amongst them and be a god as they were.

As the years went by Man waited for the gods to call to him and to welcome him to his rightful place; but always they remained silent.

One day, his impatience overflowing, Man climbed the holy mountain and, approaching the god's stronghold, he entered and stood before them.

"Give me my immortality," he said, "give me that which is mine."

The gods were angry at this intrusion—and, perhaps also, they were a little afraid that Man had dared to come and face them. They therefore sent him away from them and, closing the great gates behind him, vowed that he would never again enter their sacred courts.

And so Man was banished. The gods sent him away down the mountain with harsh and angry words because he had dared to challenge them.

Then they began to debate amongst themselves. It was true; they were holding Man's Spirit for him until the day when he would be worthy to receive it, but now—after his audacity, his impatience—they determined that it would never be his.

The gods agreed that they would destroy Man's Spirit.

To the God of the Water it appeared as a pure, flowing spring. The god poured himself upon the Spirit, but, when his torrent was spent, still the Spirit flowed unceasingly.

To the God of the Fire, the Spirit was seen as a flickering flame. The god blazed and burned but when at last, exhausted, his rage subsided, there was the Spirit flickering before him.

To the God of the Air, Man's Spirit was a gentle whisper of a breeze, no stronger than a breath. This god also felt sure that he could destroy the Spirit; so, blowing with all his might, he enveloped the breeze in his howling anger. Yet when this god at last came to rest, the breath of the Spirit still remained.

And so it was with the God of the Earth. To him Man's Spirit was as a tiny seed that he could crush into dust with the sheer weight of his body. But he again found that all his strength and size were powerless against Man's Spirit

Not one of the gods could destroy it, because it was immortal: they had made it so.

If it could not be destroyed, they determined to hide it.

But where?

Not in the ground, for they knew that Man would dig the earth until he found it.

Not in the sea: because he would dive and swim in search of it.

Not in the stars; because Man would even find a way of reaching out into the vastness of space . . .

Then the oldest and the wisest of the gods, the God of the Ether, who had been silent during all this long debate, said:

"Give it to me."

Reaching out, he took Man's flickering Spirit and covered it with his great hand and, when he opened his hand again, the Spirit had gone.

All the gods were amazed and asked him what had become of Man's Spirit.

"I have hidden it," he replied. "I have hidden it in the one place that Man will never think of looking for it."

"But, where is that?" demanded the others.

"I have hidden it," said the old god, "within Man himself."

And that is the story—and the beginning of all stories.

Later the oldest and wisest of the gods called Man back to the holy mountain and spoke to him in secret, whispering to him:
"Nothing is ever found by rushing round a circle. Be still. Find ways to become still. Then listen, at the centre, to the questions of your heart. For it is these many questions which will lead you to the few; and it is these few, strong, vital questions which will lead you to your Spirit. Trust the Questions. They are all that you need. Do not be contented with the many answers the world will offer. Listen to the Questions and follow them; they are your open sesame to the Quest. Be still, listen, your Spirit is asking for you."

*

Who am I?
Where did I come from?
Why was I born?
What is the purpose of my existence?
What happens when I die?
Why this universe?
How was it created?
What is it for?
What does this universe mean to me?
or
What am I to this universe?

*

After the years of childhood, I awake from a kind of sleep; a sleep in which I seem to have taken for granted everything that has happened to me and believed everything that I have been told. Now, waking, I find questions arising in my mind. They come usually when I am alone and quiet; they come unexpectedly.

At the time I may not notice that it is I who am asking the questions of myself.

They are deep, mysterious questions and they can be disturbing. They seem to come from a dimension beyond those that I am used to; they are questions quite outside what I normally think. I sense them to be very important and very private, as if I have been stirred by something secret deep within myself.

Occasionally I talk about these questions to my friends; but, although they may recognize what I am speaking about, they seem as mystified as I am; and, usually, we let the questions go and talk about more familiar things.

Now and again I ask older people. Some do not know, and do not seem to want to know; others try to be helpful by giving answers. But they never seem to be satisfying answers; they do not reach what I *really* want to find.

For example, when I ask who I am, they answer with my name. But that is what I am called; it is not who I am.

*

It is not difficult to ignore and forget these deep and mysterious questions because they require no immediate answers. Meanwhile, there is so much going on and my days are filled with so many activities.

The outside world is presenting a thousand other questions to be answered.

What are you going to do?

What are you going to be?

What is your ambition?

What do I want?

How am I going to fill my day?

What am I going to spend my lifetime doing?

I must find the answers to these questions. Everybody becomes something; everybody has to earn a living; everybody has to choose what they are going to be, has to choose what they are going to think about, has to choose what they want to achieve with the capabilities that they have been born with. I must stake my place in the world because I am here and I have to survive.

But how do I choose what I want to be? How do I find what I want to do?

I want to be whatever will allow me to do the things that I want to do. I want to do the things that I think I would like to do. Other-wise, I will be unhappy.

Above all, I want to be happy.

And so, to a certain extent, the deeper questions are put to one side, because they do not seem to have much to do with everyday life and its challenges. As a part of that life, I have no choice; I must become involved, accept the challenge and strive to achieve. For it is in those very achievements that I believe my happiness will be found.

And then the problems start to arise.

*

Happiness is elusive.

Difficulties, especially when other people are involved, interfere with my own desire to do just what I want to do. Worse, I find that there are many things that I must do which I would rather not do. At the same time I become aware that other people have problems; I find that they also are often troubled and unhappy.

Why should there be unhappiness and suffering?

Then I discover a new feeling, a new desire. Perhaps, after all, the most satisfying things to be and to do would be those which could be helpful to others.

So the questions multiply as the problems multiply and, if I am to cope, from where can I get help?

*

The deep questions and the feeling of wanting to help others are very much the concern of religion.

They are also the concern of philosophy, inasmuch that each of us has to develop a personal philosophy in order to cope with life.

And, as these matters are worked out largely in mind, they are also the concern of psychology.

Now, because what I decide to do has an effect on everyone around me, my "religion"—the rules by which I decide to conduct myself—and everyone else's "religion" affects every activity in all human endeavour.

So, what is religion?

*

Looking back, one of my first impressions of religion is likely to have been a religious building or a place of worship. They tend to dominate villages and towns all over the world (though not now in modern cities) and they are called churches, temples, synagogues, mosques, shrines, chapels and so on. Some are complex and ornamental; some are simple and austere. There is always a space for people to gather and nearly always a focal point for attention, usually in the form of a symbolic or human image.

Then I became aware, perhaps, of religious scriptures in people's homes and aware of religious practices among families; praying, chanting, meditating. And I noticed special men in the community, usually distinguishable by their clothing, who were called priests, rabbis, bhikkus, and so on, who officiated in the religious buildings at certain times on certain days throughout the year.

And what did I make of it all?

According to the inclinations and habits of my parents or guardians, I would have been told a little of what it was all about. Depending on how important it was to them, I would have been led into their *form* of religion and I would have been told that I was being introduced to it for various reasons. These reasons could derive from simple habit, sense of duty, gratitude, praise and, at the other end of the scale, from superstitious fear.

It is possible that if I ever questioned why I was expected to take part, I was told: "Because you must."

So if my parents or guardians were committed to a certain form of religion, it is likely that I accepted their disciplines—of going to the places of worship; of reading the scriptures; of praying, singing, chanting; of respecting the men and the women who wore the strange clothes. And I learned that my religion dictated or recommended what I should or should not do. And either I enjoyed it all or I found it boring; possibly I really loved it; or possibly it frightened me and I hated it.

*

Increasingly nowadays, to varying extents in different parts of the world, people are not introduced to the traditional religious ideas and forms. Their guidance and discipline—the rules by which they are expected to conduct themselves—come from their home and educational environment; and from those who represent the authority of the state.

*

Whatever the intensity and impact of religion in my early life, even if it was next to nothing or simply for ceremonies connected with birth, marriage and death, at some point during those years I will have gathered that the basis of all religion is the god-idea.

Man has always recognized that as a human being, a physical animal, he is subject, in the world in which he finds himself, to forces and laws over which he has no control.

In my childhood years, I am unlikely to have questioned my existence. True I will have cried when hungry, lonely or in pain. But I will not have considered that I might suddenly cease to exist. As I grow older, I still assume that the sun will rise tomorrow and that the ground will remain under my feet; but I will begin to become aware that there is the possibility of catastrophe for the individual and that there is the awesome mystery of death.

Man becomes aware, in whatever circumstances, anywhere in the world, that because of the hazards around him, life is precarious. After the "sleep" of babyhood and the "dreams" of childhood, sooner or later threats to security are borne in upon him. As an innocent, thrown into awareness of his existence in this world, how can he cope with all the challenges, threats and mysteries that confront him?

As a human being, I do seem to have been thrown in at the deep end.

When I deeply consider this situation—given that I seem to have so little information and seem so helpless in the face of such vast and mysterious problems—it is easy and understandable that I should make certain assumptions and draw certain conclusions. I must consider some of these later; but for the moment let me look at the key idea.

As a human being, I experience myself as distinct from an animal, plant or inanimate object. I observe myself to have greater intelligence, ingenuity, and so forth. But, above all, as distinct from any other entity, I seem to have a unique capacity of consciousness—to be aware that *I am*.

That naturally leads me to assume that that which caused me to be must have even greater intelligence, power and consciousness than I have.

Through my tendency to imagine and envisage things, and my inability to do so in other terms than those I am used to, I am inclined to conceive of this superior intelligence or power in the form of a "super-being". And I learn that Man calls this . . .?. . . by many names in many languages.

These names—including God, Jehovah, Allah, Brahman—imply different aspects of power and law in different religious systems. All I need to bear in mind for the moment is that, whatever the name, there can be no validity in ascribing any imaginary form to this . . .?. . . because I am talking about that which is beyond the comprehension of my mind.

It is natural, though primitive and naive, to assume the image of a "super-being" (and it is probably the only way that the idea of a superior intelligence can be conveyed to the young). If it is pursued, it gives rise to all sorts of irrelevant problems. What sex is this being? What colour? How old? Where does he/she live? And so on.

To come to any conclusion about these problems cannot be other than speculation. And that does not help me at all.

Because, in the end, I will still not know who I—the one who is subject to this imaginary deity—am.

Who am I?

Two

Who am I?

I wonder if I really know who I am even though I assume all the time that I do know?

*

In my childhood, I did not question my existence. By and large, I believed everything I was told. Quite innocently I believed the many things that I was taught—either deliberately or by accident.

I learned the language of my country, the dialect of my area and the speech-habits of my parents or guardian. I learned how to eat, how to walk, how to express myself. I copied the behaviour of my elders. I learned not to put my hand into the fire, not to bang my head, not to cut myself, not to fall off a wall or out of a tree.

In short, I learned how to survive.

As I grew up many things happened to me. Some gave me pleasure, others gave me pain. I remembered both the pleasure and the pain. In this way my behaviour was conditioned because I learned to look for the pleasure and to avoid the pain. The pursuit of the one and the fear of the other coloured my days; brightening them or darkening them, bringing enjoyment or anxiety.

At the same time I began to experience within myself certain emotions; attraction, approval, generosity, excitement, love, friendship, happiness and, conversely—rejection, criticism, meanness, depression, envy, anger, hatred, sadness . . . and so on.

I had carefree moods and I had dejected moods; I was sometimes at ease, sometimes wretched. I did not ask how these things happened, from day to day and hour to hour. I took them for granted; rather like changes in the weather.

I simply went on—preferring the one state and suffering the other.

I rarely questioned if any of this was other than it ought to be. The see-saw alternation of existence was going on all around me. The world was full of people falling out and making up, liking and disliking, arguing and agreeing, loving and fighting. It was, I believed, simply how things were.

In all this time I made certain basic assumptions—that if I was happy, it was because someone or something had made me so; and, equally, if I was sad, it was for that same reason. It seemed natural to me that if I was grateful to those who gave to me, then I must also blame those who deprived me.

*

In this way was I not beginning to know who I was?

I began by believing that I differed from other people. What made me happy did not necessarily make everyone else happy. My likes were not universal. One man's meat was another man's poison; for as many as liked "serious" music, there were an equal number who liked "popular" music—there were those who didn't like either, and equally, those who liked both. There were no hard and fast rules—only individual preferences.

If I am different from the next person, is it not natural to assume, therefore, that I am the person who holds the particular likes and dislikes peculiar to me?

Am *I* not recognizable as *me* by my persuasions? And, am *I* not *me*?

*

In all this to-ing and fro-ing, some people seemed to have more luck than others.

Some are poor and deprived; some are rich and fortunate. For those who have money, influence and power, it seems much easier to gain the ease and happiness and to avoid the misery and discomfort.

And so, very quickly, as I learned to assess advantage and disadvantage, I learned also the concept of fairness and unfairness —in relation to my situation.

"It isn't fair," was a cry that I heard over and over again. I heard myself saying it; "It isn't fair, I am unlucky."

Perhaps above all else, the witnessing of what seemed fair or unfair to me made me question what was happening. Is there any law, any justification, any reason why this is happening to me and not to him, I wondered; why am I not having this, and she is? —and so on.

Is it all accidental, I wondered—or is "someone" trying to make life difficult for me?

*

And yet—do we ever ask if it is fair to the dandelion that it does not smell like a rose; is it fair that a worm should fall prey to a bird's beak, that a thousand fish should be rudely hauled from the sea in a net, that a sparrow cannot sing like a blackbird?

Do we ever enquire about such "fairness"?

Of course we don't.

What has the worm to do with me? Or the fish? The dandelion and the rose are just different flowers, that is all. The sparrow and the blackbird were never meant to be alike.

But are we so different? Not all of us have perfect singing voices, and no amount of voice training will make them so. Not all of us are adept at sports; nor do we all have a natural leaning towards physics, or painting, sewing or higher maths! Why are some of us brainier than others? Why are some stronger? More "beautiful"? More amusing?

Is it all just a question of *luck*?

When I see the advantages enjoyed by one over another and the disadvantages suffered by one compared to another, I begin to wonder seriously what reason there can be for it all.

Is it sufficient to attribute the see-saw of existence purely to *luck*?

I soon reject the idea. We have already learned that we must make "efforts", that we must attempt to "better ourselves", that it is not right to be unhappy.

But in making ourselves happy, may we not be making someone else unhappy? Let us assume that everyone wants to get to the top of a certain tree in order that they should all be happy. It is out of the question—there isn't room at the top of that tree for all of us. But if I will be happier at the top, does it not stand to reason that I should attempt to get there—regardless of the others? What point everyone staying at the bottom, where no one is happy? Far better that a few should be happy than that everyone should remain unhappy?

And so we are back at the endless pursuit of happiness, governed by effort, which, in turn, is governed by *luck*.

The lucky few—and the unlucky many.

So long as I am lucky, all will be well. But when I am not, what then? It is not sufficient to ascribe it all to *luck*; it can't be, it is far too arbitrary; there must be a reason for it all.

And—if there is a reason, who or what is responsible?

*

As all these baffling thoughts and ideas arise in my mind, it is not difficult to see the genesis of the crucial god-idea.

What I find I need is "someone" to refer to, to be grateful to, to importune, to worship and, when necessary, to blame. Such a "someone" would take the burden off myself. What would be even better would be if this "someone" did not belong to my see-saw world of conflicting emotions, of hopes and desires with all their accompanying disappointments and despairs. What would be most useful would be a super-intelligence, a super-being, a deity perhaps.

*

A deity.

*

The moment I have proposed and then subscribed to the god-idea, many of my problems are resolved. I now have "someone" who is superior to me and, because "he" is superior, "he" is the answer to so many of my questions. "He" caused me to be. Why? For reasons of "his" own. "He" made me the way I am, with all my strengths and weaknesses. Why? For reasons of "his" own. "He" made the world and all that therein is. Why? We do not know; because "he" is superior, both in mind and in heart. "He" moves in mysterious ways . . . and the misfortunes of this world, as well as its wonders, become the "Will of Allah", the "Will of God", the "Will of Brahman", the "Will of Jehovah".

For the moment, the relief is immense! I have someone to thank, and also to blame, in any given circumstances. It is, quite simply, not my responsibility, and I do not have to worry as to who I am—if, that is, I am understanding it all correctly.

And so I seek instruction in my new-found god-idea. For I am not alone. I find that there are other people also subscribing to the worship of a deity by whatever name. They belong to differing religious traditions and they may be willing to let me join them. It is with them that I may find out more about the deity.

I discover that some people are wary about blaming the deity. It hardly seems possible, they tell me, that this deity would deliberately let us suffer; and the superstitious amongst them say that it would be risky to offend this all-powerful being in any way. Suppose, they suggest, that there is also an evil agent, a devilish power? Yes, that would be useful; or suppose, others say, Man is responsible for his own suffering?

In resolving some of my problems, I seem to have created a whole lot more!

As I begin to explore the question of religion, I find myself at once in the complexity of theological debate. It is not, evidently, just a simple matter of believing that there *is* a deity.

*

Unless I have got it wrong? Perhaps I have misunderstood what I am meant to be believing?

But, honestly, there seems to be little point in devoting a life-time to debating whether man through the ages has done right or wrong believing in this or that. What possible value can there be for me in deciding the rectitude or the absurdity of the beliefs and actions of people who are dead and gone? And of what use is it to me to conclude that others, alive today, are wise or foolish to believe or act as they do. That is simply taking me straight back to the debate for or against "serious" and "popular" music!

No.

What is most important for me is to examine what *I* can genuinely believe in. For no one can do the believing for me. I can only believe for myself.

*

It may be that I will end up rejecting the god-idea. There are many, called atheists, who do so; like the people to whom we referred earlier—those disputing that there has to be a cause of the universe —the atheist usually subscribes only to the fact of his existence and does not see any relevance or importance in the god-idea. "I am," he says, "because I am. What more do I need? I am, because I am here. When I am not here—when I am dead—then I am not. It is all perfectly simple."

To a certain extent it would be easier for me to settle for being an atheist in the contemporary world in which I live. With the growth of science, technology and urbanization, the human existence seems to become less precarious in developed countries. There is a growing tendency for man to think that he can rely on his own intelligence and ingenuity for his security. And why not? Man, the inventor, has come a significant way since the creation of the wheel; man, the doctor, has progressed from primitive healing to transplant surgery—it seems that there is nothing that man, in the end, is unable to do, once he puts his mind to it. What does one need with a deity? Is not man the deity?

And this may be so. But surely man, relying on his own devices, is only creating physical security? His mind still has to come to terms with the deep questions.

No community or state system can ultimately answer the deep

questions for me any more than a religious system can tell me what I should believe. I have to answer them for myself.

*

Myself.
Who is asking the questions?
I am.

*

Those who do accept the proposition of the god-idea are called believers. According to the degree of their understanding and their commitment to the particular system, and according to their interpretation of their experience under the discipline of that system, so they have faith in their deity—that "someone" to whom they are subject.

Some, I find, seem almost to have blind faith. They seem to have lost contact with the deep questions, and are content merely to let other people do the questioning for them. Because of them, I note that I must be wary in my pursuit of the truth. As I am introduced to the theories, arguments, persuasions and convictions of other people, I must not lose the sound of my own enquiring inner voice. I must assess for myself and put to the test of my reason and experience everything that I hear and see. It doesn't matter whether I judge others to be the tellers of truths or of lies—whether *they* be honest or deceptive; but it is essential that I look to see whether *I* am being true or lying to myself; whether *I* am being honest—or whether *I* am deceiving myself.

*

Who is it that knows when I know I am deceiving myself?

*

The search to discover whether the god-idea is valid or not might be called the religious quest and, under whatever label or banner I choose to pursue it, that quest is what religion essentially means.

Did man create the god-idea; or did the god-idea create man?

"Once upon a time, there was a man who dreamed that he was a butterfly. When he awoke, he found that he was a man. But, from that moment, he was never again quite sure that he was not a butterfly asleep—dreaming that he was a man."

*

I do not know who I am.

There was a time before my parents or guardian gave me a name —who was I then? Is it sufficient to say that I was simply "the child of my parents"? In that case, am I anything more than an extension of them? Did I, in my infancy, know this to be the case?

Or—did I simply *exist*? Was I not, in that first moment after birth, pure life; waiting to be impressed, waiting to be written on? Like this sheet of paper, perhaps, before it is covered with words. The paper does not inform (other than to say that it is "paper") only the words can do that.

But am I only a body, then, in that moment after birth; or am I a body containing a *mind*?

Is it not, so far as we can tell, *mind* that receives the countless strands of information that gradually build up the peculiarities particular to *me*? These peculiarities that become my personality that, in turn, makes me a particular person?

If the *mind* is the page on which the writing takes place—who is the writer?

If the writer is all the countless impressions that we receive—is what is written infallible?

How much is *mind* to be trusted? And, who is it that does the trusting?

Can my mind tell me, with absolute certainty, that I am a man —or does it, if pressed, admit the possibility that I am a sleeping butterfly dreaming that I am a man?

*

What we tend to overlook, in deciding whether or not there is validity in the god-idea, is—who is doing the deciding?

We will find that in all theological debate, for example, it is very rare that anyone will stop to question who is deciding, having the faith, coming to the conclusions. But what is the point of making the decision if it is not known who is to gain or lose by the deciding?

In devising his explanations of the world about him, it seems that man often leaves himself out of the account. He does so because he nearly always assumes that he knows who he is and that, therefore, it isn't worth bothering about. In other words, he is continually devising systems for the satisfaction of his bodily welfare without really considering what would be satisfying to his total self.

In my enquiry, through religious systems, into the god-idea I soon discover that one fundamental concern of all the religions is the gaining or losing of immortality. But what, I ask, can possibly be immortal when I have obvious and conclusive proof that each and every body in existence sooner or later will die?

If I assume by immortality that I am hoping to go on living forever somewhere else when I die—who or what is to go on living; who or what is it that has died?

*

I cannot afford to be vague about these questions. One of the reasons why they are so often pushed to one side is that it is doubtful that any conclusive answers will emerge. It seems that it is only in the world of my body, in the world of "things", that there are conclusions.

Yet I would still like my questions answered. In the world about me everyone is looking for and giving answers; I have got used to having them. In all fields of enquiry there seem to be specialists and experts, all of them offering lots of answers.

But with the deep questions, I have to look very carefully at what precisely I am asking; for I may well discover that cliché explanations and dogmatic answers do not satisfy me.

What can the answer be but sheer confusion if my question is not understood? But—understood by whom?

*

Let me start by understanding it myself. At least then, if I have truly listened to and understood my own question, I will be able to assess the quality of the answer I am offered.

*

And there will also be times when I am asked questions, when I am put in the role of the answerer. The same precision must still apply.

Someone may say, "I do not believe in a god" or "I do believe in a god". But who is doing the not believing or the believing; what does "believing" mean and what is meant by "god"?

When someone asks "Do you believe there is a god?", rather than answering "Yes" or "No" or "I don't know", I might pause to enquire what they mean by "god"—and why they ask. Is it because they are seeking confirmation of their own ideas? Is it because they want to challenge my ideas and persuade me with theirs? Or is it because they genuinely want to explore the question with me?

People seem to be continually trying to establish or maintain their own points of view on all sorts of matters. That may mean seeking my endorsement of their opinions, or trying to dislodge me from mine—both being an attempt to prove the validity of their own position. Or they may genuinely wish to explore the question, to see what light I may be able to throw on it. These three aspects or motives (of agreeing, disagreeing or mutually enquiring) run through all give-and-take exchanges and conversations.

Where the deep questions are concerned, the protagonist who wants to persuade and the one who wants to be persuaded will not be of much help. But the one who genuinely wants to explore is always offering an opportunity that I should not lightly dismiss.

The degree to which I will resolve the problems for myself during my life will depend upon the degree to which I make my exploration with like-minded people.

*

Whatever religious system I have been introduced to, or have encountered for myself, I will have to *make up my own mind* whether

24

to believe or not in the concepts, assertions, rules and practices of that religion.

The representatives of that religion—the priests, rabbis, bhikkus —will be committed and it is right that they should be so. Without their conviction I will not be able truly to connect with the centre of their belief—and, if I do not connect with that centre, I will not be able to assess what is there and what it is really saying to me.

After an initial period of instruction by them, however, I will be required to make a similar commitment myself. You cannot be a "believer" if you do not "believe". For a while you can pay lip-service but at some point you have to begin making up your own mind. You cannot stay on the threshold forever (or it would seem less than profitable to do so!)—sooner or later, you must either walk away or go in. (If you walk away, you are always at liberty to come back later; if you go in you can always come out again—but less than profitable to do so!); sooner or later, you must either away from the threshold or across it—there are many variations or degrees. Different religions make different demands. I may be attracted or repulsed by so many aspects and considerations.

But—and this again is often overlooked—what is going on in the process?

*

As I awake from the dreams of childhood, I begin to become aware that I have to take my place in the world. Having accepted for so long the beliefs, practices and attitudes of my environment —home, parents, friends, school, teachers, and so on—I begin to think for myself. And I begin to experience unfamiliar feelings and emotions. Increasingly I have things of my own—private thoughts, secret longings, special possessions. Though I may not realize it, I am beginning to emerge as an individual; and I begin to desire independence.

Perhaps, occasionally, I wonder who I am; but mainly the process is one of staking out my own territory—holding certain beliefs and opinions, behaving in certain ways, pursuing certain activities, making special relationships, desiring and owning certain

25

prized objects. All these things I call mine and their sum total somehow constitutes me. To the world about me, they are the things by which I am identified. "He does this, she does that; he believes this, she believes that; he owns this, she owns that; he is like this, she is like that"; and so on.

Creating this personal territory is essential if I am to take my place in the world and be recognized as myself. It could be called "the forming of personality" and it is a very time- and energy-consuming endeavour.

The creating, maintaining and modifying, enhancing and extending of the image I project on the world about me could be seen as the motive power behind most of what I think and do. The image I create is very important to me. Perhaps it is to everyone? Do we not all continually want recognition and, preferably, admiration?

The important point about this process, as far as the exploration of this book is concerned, is that we are seeking to establish our identity *in the eyes of the world*.

But when all has been said and done in my life, even if I have achieved widespread fame or notoriety, even if the world at large can immediately say: "Oh, there goes so-and-so . . ."—is that enough? Has any of it helped me to know my real identity—who I really am?

*

The deep questions stir.

All these things have been achieved—and it is very right and proper that they should have been if they have been useful to me or to anyone else; the world knows many things about me; I may even have learned many things "about" myself.

But—who is it who has achieved them? Who is it who has learned?

*

If I am sure there is a deity, or if I am sure there is not, or if I do not know or care—who am I who has decided so? And does it matter one iota to such a deity, if one exists, whether I decide one way or another? Clearly if there is no deity, it is entirely matter-less —but I'll only know that, if I know the deity doesn't exist!

It is in the exploration of the deep questions—not in the so-called answers or opinions—that a different process is taking place. The penetration to the heart of the religious question is the search for my real self.

*

Who am I?

*

Going back in my memory as far as I can, remembering some of the things that have happened to me, I can see that at some point in the past of my life I began to become me as the world sees me. *At the same time "I" began.* I can see how, in my exchanges with the world, I began to emerge and form as a person in my own right. In this sense I began to become me, presumably, from the moment after I was born. But if "I" cannot remember being born, and certainly cannot remember being conceived inside my mother, then when did "I" really begin?

If "I" began with the first remembered thing, where was "I" before that?

Where did "I" come from?

Three

Where did I come from?

Wherever it was, it is certain that I am here now.

If I am in any doubt about that, I have only to pinch myself! The pain that my body registers tells me that I am here. Presumably, if my body was dead it wouldn't feel a thing—and my body is mine. It was my first possession. It doesn't belong to anyone else. Only *I* can feel its pain.

*

So . . . "here I am" . . . looking the way that I do; with certain attributes, peculiar to me; with certain achievements, particular to me; with certain possessions acquired by me. I have my identity and my territory in the world.

I have a definite sense of being me.

Furthermore, other people are constantly confirming and maintaining my sense of myself. When someone says to me: "Hello, good to see you . . ." I am the first to agree that it is me that they are seeing. They are confirming absolutely, that I am here now. They see me and recognize me.

Well—they certainly see and recognize my face, my body—the attributes peculiar to me.

*

The other day, upon the stair,
I met a man who wasn't there.
He wasn't there again today,
I do so wish he'd go away.

28

That is the stuff of fairy tales and ghost stories. In order "to be there" he must be embodied.

If, that is to say, I am my body?

*

But when I become involved in thoughts and activities, I often lose my sense of myself. And when I am asleep, it is as though I cease to exist altogether.

Where have I gone, I wonder, when I am asleep?

*

I go to sleep and the next event of which I am aware is that I am awake again. "What time is it?" I ask and I may be surprised to find that the clock has moved on.

Sometimes when I am asleep, I dream. But did I know that I was dreaming at the time, or, am I only aware that "I had a dream" when I wake up?

Where was I, while I was asleep?

*

If I am in a room where someone else is sleeping—where has that person "gone to"? I am able to see his or her body; so they are still there, physically. But if for them, one moment they are awake *before* sleep and the next moment, seemingly, they are awake *after* sleep—where did they "go" in between those two events?

Did they go anywhere? As far as I am concerned the answer is "No". I saw the sleeping body—it never went anywhere.

But the person, on the other hand, did NOT see their body lying there—or they were not aware of it.

What is it, I wonder, that can lose this awareness?

*

When I am awake, at times I am confused and bewildered; at other times I am confident and sure of what I am doing.

Sometimes I am pleased with myself; sometimes I am thoroughly displeased—to the point of disliking myself.

Who is it that I like or dislike and who is it who is doing the liking and disliking?

Are there perhaps two of me inside me—one constantly judging the other?

*

As I begin to establish myself, as I begin to emerge as an individual in my own right, it is almost as if "I am being born".

Of course, my body was born many years before and, since then, I have thought and done many things. But it does seem that all that time and experience was a preparation for becoming conscious of "being myself".

It is at this point that the deep questions arise in the mind. And I discover that these questions are very much concerned with my new-found awareness of myself—my individuality.

*

Who is it who is asking these questions?

Is it me? How can it be? Who am I asking? I am asking me!

Could it be that there is more than one of these persons I call "me"?

Perhaps there are many of these "me"s?

If there are many "me"s, is there perhaps, deep within—among the many "me"s that make up the idea of me—one single original me? The first me? The "real I".

Perhaps it is this "real I" who asks the deep questions?

*

But I do not want to spend all my time looking inwards, considering who I am; there is also the looking outwards to experience the world and to consider my relationship with it, as it affects me from minute to minute, day to day.

Here again it is all rather complicated. My happiness seems to depend on being able to do the things I want to do and have the things I want to have. Happiness seems to depend on the fulfilment of my desires. But, I am required also to do things I do not want

o do and there are even certain things that I want to do that I am
not allowed to do; and things that I want to have that I am not
allowed to have.

It is all most confusing; like playing a game—without any
rules.

I discover that there are rules; of course there are. Without
rules there can be no structure or conduct of the game. Without
rules there is only chaos and no possibility of establishing the game;
you must know what you are allowed to do and what you are banned
from doing before play can commence.

In order that I may survive and so maintain the sense of myself,
it is necessary that I should be introduced to these rules.

*

The rules seem to derive from several sources.

At first it is my parents or guardians who say what I may or may
not do, what I may or may not have and what I ought and ought not
to do and have. Some of these rules are easy to accept; if I try to
touch a flame when I have been told not to, then I very soon learn
why I was given the rule. It is to my benefit to obey such a rule—
and there are many of them. They are obviously for my own
physical protection and safety.

But some instructions are more obscure to me. I do not see the
reason for them so readily.

So: I learn that some of the rules are clearly for my own protection
and welfare; then I see that others—and these are rules that I may
find more restrictive—are really to do with the protection and the
welfare of the community in which I live. And there are a further
set of rules that are to do with the security and survival of the
state to which my community belongs.

As I am a part of my community so I see that I am also a part,
however small, of the state: and that what happens to the state
will affect me.

At the same time I am introduced to the fact that nature, other
people, other communities and other states are, on occasions,
threats to my survival. Perhaps I accept all this as a part of life—

31

but it is not comforting to begin to realize that there are elements in my environment that are hostile and that they may do me harm without any apparent provocation.

I can understand that if I do something that harms someone else, then I should be prepared to face reprisals; but that something or someone should, without compunction, harm me . . .

And there are some rules that are to do with "morals" and "ethics". These are most difficult to understand. They seem to derive, directly or indirectly, from the religion or religions to which I and those around me subscribe.

These rules could be said to have a general theme; that it is "bad" to be "selfish" and that it is "good" to be "self-less".

When I enquire, I am told that to be "selfish" is to do something that I personally want to do, regardless of how it may affect other people; to think only about me and not to allow the affairs of other people to stand in the way of my achieving my desires.

To be "self-less" is seen particularly in denying my own desires and serving instead the needs of other people or the community or state.

In religious terms being "self-less" is usually seen as serving the god-idea and being "selfish" is acting contrary to the god-idea and to the beliefs and disciplines that this involves.

*

It is "good" to be "self-less", I learn, it is "bad" to be "selfish".

*

This concept of "good" and "bad" is very subtle. Once I have been introduced to it I very soon find that I am judging every event and action in its light.

The subtlest form of the "good/bad" rule comes to me through my religion's injunctions. I learn who I should honour, respect and obey; how I should conduct myself, both in my exchanges with the world and also in my private behaviour. My sexual activities my desires—sometimes even the food that I eat—are all subject to these rules. In order that they should be observed and obeyed they

nclude, to varying degrees, threats of punishment for wrong-doing
and the promise of rewards for goodness.

*

If, in my childhood, I have been influenced by religion, the
threat of punishment will have made me fearful of "committing
sin"; and, at the same time, the promises of reward will have
prompted me to do "good deeds".

However, as I grow older, I learn that there is a certain artificiality
and confusion in the definitions of good and bad. Sometimes the
good deeds are done with all kinds of subtle, selfish motives—
especially to be thought well of by others, or because I want the
reward.

But only I will know these subtle variations—and often they
escape even me.

Sometimes I do good deeds and do not get a reward; and sometimes I commit sin and do not get punished.

I begin to wonder who does the rewarding and the punishing?
And I wonder what form the rewards and punishments I am seeking
or avoiding will take?

This question is further confused by the fact that in most religious
systems the glittering heavens and the terrible damnations are not
to be awarded until "after life". In some mysterious way, it appears
that a tally is kept of our creditable behaviour and our mis-
demeanours and that the appropriate fate will be administered
after we are dead and in another place.

*

Over questions of morality and how I conduct myself in relation
to other people, "learning the rules", I find that there is another
crucial factor—the "heart".

It becomes apparent in my growing experience of life that my
actions and responses are affected in *two* ways; not only how I *think*,
but how I *feel*.

I come to associate thinking with the head and feeling with
the heart. With the former there is a "working out of things";

B   33

with the latter there seems to be a kind of "instinctive response".

In my looking outwards at the world, I find the heart responding according to my mood. In a good mood, I may experience the heart "going out" to people and things.

"My heart went out to . . ."

When this happens I experience sympathy, pity, gratitude, joy —and love . . . spontaneously, without thinking about it.

It is difficult for me to define what these experiences are; are they sensations, feelings . . .? What is happening to me when I am experiencing them?

Life starts to become serious as these new *emotions* move me and I try to cope with them.

*

Why am I feeling like this?

What is the feeling?

Why am I behaving in this way? What is the reason for my action? What is the reason for the way that others are reacting towards me?

*

Suddenly, the playing is over and my little world of games gives way to new horizons, new ambitions, new challenges. I begin to look for ideals and perfections. I begin to idolize and to strive to emulate the excellent; competition becomes very much a part of my life. Those people who represent perfection and excellence in the activities and goals that attract me become my heroes, my heroines, my champions and even my idols.

I can actually grow to worship the person who seems to have achieved what I am seeking to achieve.

There are so many categories here—according to the type of person I am. For some it may be at the level of the physical—to do with skill, beauty and expertise in movement; for some it might be in the realm of knowledge—scientific and technical craft, ingenuity and inventiveness; or in the realm of the arts—in music, literature, painting, acting, singing, craftsmanship. Or it may be in the field of adventurous, romantic or dedicated lives—explorers, war-heroes, champions of causes.

Each of us finds our idols and then we worship.

What we identify with has so much to do with what we want to be and do ourselves; and how we would like to appear to other people.

It could be said that, as we begin to "become ourselves", we begin to create.

＊

As *I* emerge—so I begin to create "myself".

＊

And *sex* begins to play its part; the one sex fashioning itself in many subtle ways in relation to the other sex.

So, from the world around me, I find in those I admire the standards I would like to attain for myself. Immediately I am inviting the possibility of frustration and the fear of failure. In that moment I come up against apparent weaknesses and shortcomings in myself and, at the same time, resistance and obstacles placed in my way by other people.

＊

There isn't room at the top of the tree for all of us.

＊

Being thwarted in my designs and ambitions, I learn anger, criticism and dislike. I become unreasonable and I do things that later I may regret. I begin to resent the tribulations of my life and, if I am not careful, the resentment turns inwards and I begin to feel cut off and isolated from the world around me.

＊

The opening up of the heart in love and gratitude, and the failures of my particular endeavours which bring unhappiness and despair, both find scope for expression and relief in the religious context. But only, of course, if I am already inclined and accustomed to the religious habit.

The sun is shining, people are kind to me, there are things to look forward to, I am succeeding in some task—then I feel enthusiastic, elated and "all's well with the world". My heart goes out and I am thankful to the deity who permitted it all. I sing praise and gratitude; for it is good to be alive and it is easy to love everything and everyone around me . . .

But on the other hand . . .

Things are going wrong, people are unkind to me, I am fearful of what may happen, I am failing in something that I have set out to do, I seem beset by problems, I feel anxious and despondent. Then my heart becomes heavy and I turn to the deity for comfort. More; I begin to feel desperate, life may not seem worth living, I may feel I need help—then, if I have accepted the god-idea and I am accustomed to religious practice, I may turn and implore the deity for assistance . . .

I see here a fundamental duality in my affairs. Either things seem to be going with me or against me; and I feel a "going out" or a "withdrawing in".

*

But why should it be so? What can I do about it?

*

As I enjoy and suffer this constant alternation, I notice several attitudes in myself.

Firstly, I tend to think of the suffering as being unfair. What have I done to deserve these setbacks? Unless I decide to give up completely, which happens to some people later in life, I am inclined to think that I am an undeserving victim of fate and other people's lack of understanding and consideration for me. However, I have a determination which persists in assuming that it must be possible to devise a life for myself in which there will be the minimum of suffering and the maximum of happiness. I instinctively hope that at some time in the future there will be no unhappiness, no suffering. At first this tends to be my idea of the perfect situation; then I want others to join me in my vision and especially one other person with whom I may share it. Later, if my ideas are expansive

36

and I find they coincide with the ideas of others, we may join to-gether in an attempt to achieve the perfect situation. In this way causes and ideologies are born. (And the trouble starts when the adopted causes and ideals of one group are opposed by the causes and ideals of other groups, and one group tries to force its vision on another.)

Secondly, and disconcertingly contrary to the above, I may see that whatever my planned ideal situation, things have a habit of going wrong and people let me down. If I survey the history of human endeavour, and the current examples around me, I see a bewildering array of compromise; of violence, born of frustration, greed, prejudice, boredom, dogmatism, wishful thinking . . . Furthermore, so many of those who have apparently succeeded—having gained certain power, wealth and fame—do not seem to be satisfied and are continually having to struggle to enhance and hold on to what they do have.

The third attitude that I notice in myself falls between these two poles—of striving to succeed and slipping towards failure. It is a definite alternative—to seek a diversion from, or a suspension of, either of the other two activities.

To "escape".

One form of escape is to be entertained—television, theatre, reading, music, hobbies, games, whatever I enjoy. In any way that I may seek to be entertained I am diverted for the time being from the concern of either striving to succeed or resisting failure.

Another form involves my taking into my body substances that will relieve my inner tensions.

Then there is the escape into unconsciousness—the losing of my awareness of myself and my predicament in either sleep or, ulti-mately, in death.

*

Is it any wonder, when I survey all this, that I sometimes pause to ask—"What is the point of it all?"

*

37

But—if I pause for a moment; now, if I pause I may hear other questions.

Who is it who is involved in the succeeding, in the failing and in the escaping?

Where did I acquire my ideas of what is success or failure?

How did I come by my image, however vague, of the perfect situation that I am currently striving to achieve?

Who is it who is glad to be entertained? Who wishes to escape?

If I quietly consider these questions—is there not a strange, illusory quality about the ideas that I have acquired?

It is almost as though I have been fooled into some strange play in which I am required to perform a part that I do not really want.

Am I the only one who thinks like this?

Does everyone else know what they are doing and why they are doing it?

Am I peculiar and alone in my utter, baffled confusion?

Or do you, also, not really understand?

Are you, also, going along in a "cloud of unknowing"?

Who is deluding who?

Can anyone tell me?

*

Please let there be somewhere a like-minded person; another confused, baffled, unknowing someone with whom I may communicate and share my bewilderment.

Otherwise—am I absolutely alone?

*

The other day, upon the stair,
I met a man who wasn't there.
He wasn't there again today . . .

*

One thing that I realize is that nothing stands still, nothing is constant, everything changes. There is birth, living, death; a coming into existence, a continuing and an ending of all things.

Perhaps I am so involved in the business of living and competing, that I do not think very much about my own birth and my own death. Indeed, there are those who would tell me that it is maudlin and unhealthy to consider my death. "Live for today," they say, "let tomorrow take care of itself."

I do know that in some ways I am changing all the time, both physically and mentally. And yet—for all I believe that I am changing, and for all that other people tell me that I am changing —there is something "within" me that never seems to change.

Look at a photograph of yourself, taken years ago. People may say, "This was you when you were such an age . . ." Can it really be me? That stranger, staring out of the photograph, that I don't really recognize at all? But; yes, it was me—and how I have changed! It certainly isn't the face or the body that I see now when I look in the mirror. And, if I consider further, the things that I think about and do *now* were of no concern to that person *then*. It is a stranger, that person who was me; a completely different being.

And yet . . . if I can recall when the photograph was taken . . . it was a hot summer day perhaps, there wasn't a cloud in the sky . . . If I can remember the situation when the photograph was taken—then I will be remembering what it was like looking out from that person's eyes. And, strangely, is not the sense of "being there" *then* not exactly the same as the sense of "being here" *now*? Is not the inner sense of "being me" the same in both situations? A great deal has changed—but I remember I was there then, and I know that I am here now. And, somehow, despite all the changes, there seems to be no time in between—certainly, the passing of the years is meaningless.

Could it be that the "I" that was there then is the same as the "I" that is here now?

But that would mean that "I" never grows any older.

Could it be that everything about *me* changes, but that "*I*" do not change at all?

*

This is a mystery that I cannot ignore. I come back to it many times. It does not immediately answer where I came from when I

39

was born, nor does it tell me where I go when I die. But I sense that it is a vital clue to the understanding of who *I* am now.

*

Perhaps, also, it has something important to contribute to the question of religion and a full understanding of the pros and cons of the god-idea. For, if the "I" were to be constant, then it seems possible that that same "I" would do the understanding through me.

And so—another question arises:

Why was I born?

Four

Why was I born?

Is it sufficient to explain the phenomenon of birth simply as the consequence of my parent's copulation? Without them I learn that I would not have been born—but does their physical act sufficiently explain my individual, independent existence?

In worldly terms, and by that I mean also the "natural" world, this would seem to be adequate reasoning. My individual life is as much the result of the fertilization of the female egg by the male sperm as is the individual life of a fish, a bird, or even an insect. In this respect my existence is no more special than most life-forms existing in nature.

It is after birth that the complications start.

For a while, being entirely dependent upon my parents or guardian, I am as much a creature of nature—a created thing—as is the kitten, the puppy, the fledgling bird, or the baby elephant. But already a differentiation has taken place. I, and all creatures like me, am dependent on my natural parents for support and sustenance in my infancy. Without some guardian it is unlikely that I will survive. But the newly created being in the fish and insect worlds is soon left to its own devices; and, in the plant world—except in man's cultivated garden—seeds are carried on the wind to settle and possibly survive entirely at the whim of chance.

The final and most significant difference arises when I reach the age of about seven. By this time I can see that I have already acquired the first simple rules of survival and I am embarking upon the more complicated course of learning the subtle rules peculiar to man. These rules are not based upon instinct and natural movement alone, but are to do with the thinking out of things in the head and the complex feelings and desires of the heart.

If an animal is hungry, it will seek food; so will I. But does an animal desire elaborate concoctions to stimulate and gratify the taste buds? Does an animal learn to read, write, express itself artistically and so on?

It is in this area that my question—Why was I born?—becomes pressingly relevant.

*

What, I wonder, first prompted primitive man to crawl deep into the heart of a cave and, with remarkable talent, draw pictures of the animals he hunted for food on to the rough rock?

Perhaps it was the first indications of a deep, inarticulated need in him? Perhaps it was the desire to leave behind him some record of his existence?

Or was it the first flickering expression of his religious other-self? Was he beginning to emerge as a created being set apart from the rest of nature—a being that was beginning to question *why*?

In those strangely beautiful and even touching cave drawings, are we perhaps looking at the first, tentative emergence of the inner nature of man, the first stirrings of the deep questions?

Perhaps I will never know—not as a certainty. In order to know I would have to *be* that first, primitive man. I can only guess.

*

As the questions begin to arise in me, I very naturally turn my attention to consider the religious systems that have grown up in my world. It is a natural turn because they present something of a challenge; they are, apparently, set apart from the complexity of worldly affairs.

The religious phenomenon and my own inner questioning have a likeness of quality. The religious buildings in the community stand for a dimension of life that is concerned with the "deeper" or "higher" aspects of human existence; a life, seemingly, not involved with the worldly strivings for physical and mental survival, comfort and accomplishment. (Though, when I look closer, I will discover that all over the world and throughout history the religious influence has sought to involve itself in community and worldly affairs. Whether this should be so, specially without invitation, is a debate in itself. But I must be wary of such side-tracks; I soon discover that they lead me straight into the confusion that I am trying to resolve.)

The official representatives of the religions are present in greater or lesser numbers according to either the wealth of the religious establishments or the interest and requirement of the people. (Does the survival and relevance of the religious establishment depend on inspiration from "above" through its representatives or from the requirements of the people "below"? This again is a debate, but perhaps it will become apparent to me later that it is not, nor has it ever been, an "either-or" situation; perhaps the two aspects are inextricably and reciprocally one? You cannot have one without the other; an inspired teacher is as nothing without an interested student; an interested student is nowhere without an inspired teacher.)

If I leave aside religion's involvement in temporal matters— political, economic and social—at least for the moment, then the religious image has among its assets the advantages of comparative permanence, stability, continuity and security. Its importance may fluctuate from time to time and from place to place but, in the main, its threads, in their various forms, have woven continuously through the tapestry of human history. Certainly it is debatable whether man invented religion for his own satisfaction, but there can be no doubt that it has fulfilled its human requirements—indeed, it still does. In general, the forms of religion have always been accepted as an essential ingredient in human society, even though at times the different forms have sought to suppress and eliminate each other. (But are those unseemly activities the fault of the religion or the men who are interpreting it in inappropriate ways?) Now, in modern times, as a result of the effects of science, technology and

43

industry, certain materialistic ideologies, gathering strength in many parts of the world, have elected to dispense with religion altogether and actively discourage it in their societies. This last development seems very significant. Does it not indicate a crucial point in human evolution? Does it represent a foolhardy and disastrous movement which will result in men being no more than well-organized colonies like ants, simply surviving and reproducing themselves? Or does it signify progress, in that men are facing the facts of existence and are beginning to regulate themselves intelligently and be responsible for themselves?

*

Am I alive at a time when, regardless of past evidence, the god-idea is no longer viable or even useful to man?

*

The atheistic materialist might argue: "Yes, man did invent the god-idea when he was primitive, ignorant and superstitious. Now he is growing up and can with his intelligence conduct his own affairs with increasing confidence. The god-idea is no longer necessary nor relevant. When you are a child, for example, you believe in magic—but, later, you put away such childishness and believe in the laws of cause and effect."

The religious man might then counter: "Certainly man has advanced in learning and ingenuity. But he is still subject to the same ultimate limitations. He cannot create life and he cannot avoid death. Faced by such incomprehensible enigmas, how can he possibly believe himself to be self-sufficient and independent?"

I begin to see that whether states and societies are right or wrong to maintain or dispense with the god-idea can have no absolute answer—certainly not as far as any man living today can judge. But, if there is to be an evolution of human thought, will it not come about through the polarization of these two, opposing views? Never before in history has such a fundamental dichotomy revealed itself so starkly on a world-wide scale. Never before has it been so

44

crucial for the individual to examine what is going on and to try and understand it.

*

I must ask, yet again, where am I in all this? For, in the end, only I can make up my own mind.

This may not be the answer to the question "Why was I born?"—but, being born, it at least offers a good reason for "going on living".

I am here in order that I may discover for myself what I can or cannot believe. No one else can make that discovery for me.

It matters not what the neighbour, the friend, the parent, the teacher, the monarch, the milkman, the prime minister, the wife, the president, the boy friend, or the priest believes. Ultimately, as death intercedes, I am only left with what I honestly believe. It is then of little use to me to rely on what I have been persuaded to believe, whatever rag-bag and patched-up package that might be, however glorious and high flown—I can only trust what I have realized for myself.

This does not mean that I must take no account of the propositions and arguments—what others think and say and what others have thought and said through the ages will be essential food to me. Nor does it mean that I will not express my point of view and be an influence on others as they will be on me. Far from it.

Providing that I am not persuaded against my judgement and that they are not persuaded against theirs, then here is the possibility of understanding—for me.

*

This prospect, this call or exhortation to the individual to realize his own real nature, strength and independence, is not new; there have always been religious men and philosophers who have understood it. But perhaps now we are entering an era in human history when it will not be just the isolated few who will understand it? Perhaps many people are reaching beyond the historical concern of the masses for physical survival?

Certainly, on the evidence of the world about me, many are

seeming to question as I do. Is not the voice of dissent heard in most lands today? Are not more and more people turning away from the complexities of modern living and seeking alternative life styles which will afford them the peace and time in which to explore the meaning of their existence?

*

Would I be greedy if I fully realized that what I have or covet in excess of what I need corrupts *me*?

Would I hate and be angry if I fully realized that these emotions sap *my* energy and that I am causing *myself* suffering?

Would I be lazy if I realized that in being so I was rotting and failing to see my purpose?

Would I be proud if I clearly saw that the estimation, envy and admiration of others ultimately counted for nothing?

If I could see the perspective of my whole life and the ending of it, would I concern myself with the trivial and the transitory?

*

Freed from the burden of maintaining my image in the eyes of the world and acquiring that which, ultimately, I cannot keep; freed from putting my trust in fallible and inconstant things—then, maybe, I would realize the real nature of what is going on and the real nature of myself?

If this development of understanding were to happen on an increasing scale—and I am persuaded that it could be so, for there does seem evidence of it in the behaviour of some of the other people in my world—then mankind would become as different in its nature as it is now so different from the first primitive man who crept into his cave and drew that first simple drawing.

Nothing stands still and remains constant—why then should I believe that my generation will?

I can remain in my thinking and activity just an extension of my past. Or I can listen to the deep questions that disturb me with their insistence and with their refusal to be fobbed off with shallow, trite answers.

And I am not alone in this—am I?

When I discover how many others are seeking and questioning, each in their own way, then I begin to see what is really going on.

Here I stand—right in the middle of a revolution!

For so long we have joked about it—"come the revolution" has become one of our stock phrases.

What revolution?

A revolution in man's history—a renaissance of man himself.

In this way man would become truly religious for I would become "bound-again" (Latin: *re:ligio*) to who I really am.

*

Now returning to the survey of the religious phenomenon, I can see that the religious institution represents a challenge which I must consider if I am no longer content with the mundane concerns of my life.

If I am bewildered by the problems confronting me, by the disconcerting uncertainties, inconstancies and arguments and by the ever-changing scene in which nothing seems "worth it", then I can turn to religion as something reassuring, dignified and apart.

The world's traditional religions have survived over a period of many centuries and despite war, disease and natural catastrophe, they are still here, with, nominally at any rate, millions of adherents.

They all offer messages of help and salvation, healing and comfort. They all invite the vulnerable, ailing and fallible human being to surrender himself to the wiser and ancient deity or deities.

Within the history of the religious experience I hear about the inspiration and strength it has been to countless people throughout the centuries. I see and learn that the religious context has been the basis for some of the most valuable and revered artistic achievement—in architecture, writing, music, sculpture, painting and many other art and craft forms of expression.

When I witness the ritual—the colour, movement and sanctity of the festivals; and I witness the services and offices which have altered little over the decades—the reassuring repetition of word and gesture that punctuate the days and years, marking the ever-repeating cycles of the seasons; and I see the ceremonies, practices and observances associated with the human cycle of birth, marriage and death; the symbolic rites of initiation and departure, of sowing and harvesting, of emergence and disappearance, the fate of man inextricably linked with the laws of nature . . .

When I witness all this, if I am sensitive, then I tend to get a sense of myself as being temporary, brief, insignificant . . .

When I walk into a holy building, I realize that it has been, and possibly still is, highly valued by many people. No one—I doubt even the most atheistic—can entirely ignore the atmosphere in such a place.

All this must be taken into account when posing the question of religion.

The experiencing of a holy place—the space, serenity, furnishings, images, chanting, praying, and so on—can have a variety of differing effects on people. The atmosphere can produce a sense of humility, peace, inspiration, gratitude . . . even fear of an awe-ful kind. It is, perhaps, a mixture of any of these factors that draws a person towards religion; to seek refuge in the womb-like space, to surrender to "higher powers", to focus and regulate life around the measured repetition of rituals and disciplines.

As distinct from the vagaries and fluctuations of the world's affairs, religion seems to give relief and a sure foundation for everyday living to the believer. Unlike most other human institutions, it is unlikely to "let him down".

All—and it is arguably a sizeable all—that is required of religious devotees is that they yield to the disciplines and beliefs of their chosen religion and, in return, will be given a strict code of consequential behaviour that will guide them and govern them from the moment of acceptance right to the grave.

It may not always be easy to accept the dictums of the religion, but with them comes a sense of purpose and aim to endeavour.

Even when things seem to be going hopelessly "wrong", the religious person, strong in his devotion, rests in the belief that the "wrongness" is the will of the deity and that the deity is caring for him, even if that caring is at times obscure.

48

Common to all such religious emotion and practice, wherever in the spectrum of motive a particular adherent may lie, is the essential ingredient that "it takes you out of yourself"—

But—and, again, it is a large *but* for the questioning individual— *Who* is being taken out of *what*?

*

Closely linked with the emergence of my "becoming and being myself" is my search for perfection and the ideal. I may be looking for this in many ways but, whatever form this search takes, what I am looking for is something that I can believe in, trust, worship and love.

For some, the god-idea—the fulcrum of religious teaching— becomes the focus of attention. If I conceive that the deity (or deities) is the creator of the universe, if I invest that deity with infallibility and maintain that the deity governs all things for their own good, and if I accept that the deity is capable of judging, rewarding, punishing—then what better representation of perfection and ideal could there be? I can surrender to such omnipotence while I live—and I can also surrender to that omnipotence when, in due time, I reach my end; when I die.

*

But is it so easy to believe in, to trust, to worship and to love an abstract concept? If there is to be this "object" of adulation, then I am inclined to want to give such an object an image or a form. Can I do this with any conviction? The world has given this concept of absolute perfection so many different images. If my deity is the creator of the universe, how can someone else have quite a different creator of this same universe?

If, as I am told, I cannot *see* my deity—except, apparently, in very rare and "heightened" circumstances—at least I can *speak* to such a being. But if I am to speak with any effect, then there must be a hearing and, therefore, there is presumably an ear? The ear must have a mechanism . . . and back I come to the impasse of having to assume form where I have no absolute evidence or justification for doing so.

*

The religious person says to me: "But it is all so simple. Keep it simple. Don't complicate it all with your questions. Simply believe . . ."

And so, perhaps, I decide that I will pray. I kneel down, as I have been taught, and I say my prayers. But later—if I do not *believe*—I get up again and, with irritation, I declare: "It's no good. I am only talking to myself."

Why am I denied what others appear to have?

What is this believing?

What is happening when other people believe that they can speak to the deity or when they are convinced that the deity is speaking to them?

*

I find that there are a number of extraordinary records about this in the annals of religious testament; but they all largely depend on having to ascribe human attributes to the deity—even if it be only a mysterious voice that is heard.

Having not as yet been chosen for such visitations and signs, I must decide for myself whether there is any justification for assuming an anthropomorphic deity.

If I make the assumption, then I can see that a considerable number of problems and obstacles will be resolved. I will be able to visualize my deity's attributes, characteristics, modes of activity, motives, and so on, in human terms. I will be able to assume that through some invisible method the deity is able, possibly through subsidiary intermediaries, to take a direct hand in my affairs and in the affairs of man. It will be no problem for me to say, "The deity does this and that, approves of this and disapproves of that, will reward this and punish that". I will be able to assert that my deity, be he God, Allah, Jehovah, Brahman, is like this or like that and I will speak his name with confidence and familiarity. If I

50

believe that "he" is on my side in any endeavour then I will have great courage to succeed and if necessary defeat the other side. My deity, given shape, qualities and a name, will be as a friend to me; someone with my very best interests in his heart.

On the other hand, if I am reluctant to visualize an anthropomorphic deity, I have other alternatives. I can, simply, ignore the problem and yet continue to believe that in some mysterious way the speaking and hearing continues to exist. Yet again, I can actively reject the god-idea and accept instead the consequences of being an atheist. Or I can shelve the problem for the time being, neither accepting nor rejecting, determining that I will consider the whole question later "when I have more time".

Or I could reject the idea of a man-like deity and open my mind to the possibility that maybe I have been thinking entirely along the wrong lines.

Perhaps the god-idea is not a simple question of *my* deciding to believe that there is or is not *a* deity, as if there has to be some celestial entity somewhere at large in outermost space? Who am I to conceive and decide such things?

Perhaps I am being far too simplistic, primitive and literal about the whole matter? Perhaps I have not even begun to consider the matter correctly?

*

Clearly, all this activity of considering is going on in *my mind*.

But just suppose that my mind cannot possibly comprehend the deity? Perhaps it can accept only that it is subject to something, some force, beyond its understanding?

*

I believe that I am vulnerable and mortal. It would be a comfort to think that I could surrender myself to a deity "out there somewhere". It might enable me to accept my vulnerability and my mortality. But would it alter anything? Would it make me invulnerable and immortal?

My body will always be vulnerable and will surely die. My mind is also vulnerable; I can be hypnotized, brainwashed, hallucinated, drugged, inebriated, go mad, have a break-down, suffer psychotic, schizophrenic or other mental disorders. Where am I if I go out of my mind?

And where is my mind if my body dies?

*

Perhaps I am in danger of taking my mind for granted in much the same way that I can see I take my body for granted?

My mind speaks to me of being invulnerable and immortal? But how can I be invulnerable or immortal if I do not know who it is who is to be invulnerable or immortal?

*

Why should I be aware of the concept of immortality? For I am aware of it. I know what I think I am talking about. Is immortality an acquired concept? If so, where did I acquire it from, or from whom? Someone once, somewhere, first acquired the concept. Where did it come from?

Is it reasonable that I can only have been made aware of the possibility of immortality because it is feasible *in fact*? Or, to put it the other way round, would it be unreasonable that I should be capable of conceiving it without actually being able to realize it?

Does *my mind* play complicated tricks on me? From whence does it acquire its *ideas*? What are "ideas"? Until now, it has seemed that *my mind* stored impressions. How can it contain an impression of immortality—if immortality cannot and does not exist? Can *my mind* lie to me? I certainly can lie to myself. But why should my mind bother? And, what is a lie, if it is not a misrepresentation of the truth?

If there is *any* truth in the idea of immortality—how can I realize it?

*

Perhaps to realize it, there must be a going much deeper? To the very depth of my mind, even, and . . . beyond, where my mind cannot reach?

Perhaps there is a link between the deep questions of my inner nature, the concept of immortality and my ability to postulate the god-idea?

What a challenging and fascinating possibility!

Perhaps, if it is unjustifiable to think of an anthropomorphic deity "out there somewhere", then there can be no possibility of locating, in physical terms, that which is given the name of God, Allah, Brahman or Jehovah?

Perhaps whatever is asking the deep questions in me is related to whatever suggests the concept of immortality?

*

Now—at this moment—I notice my mind tiring. It seems that when I press it to extremes it wants to give up! To stop, to rest, to turn to other more tangible considerations, to more amusing and entertaining pursuits, to more familiar things.

Can it be that my mind, also, desires to be "taken out of itself"?

Is it desperate for a rest in the same way that my body becomes desperate after prolonged physical exercise?

Because so much of my searching and activity, as I pursue the religious question, will be taking place in my mind—then it seems obvious that I must find ways of giving it a rest. However, taxing my mind does not necessarily make me physically tired—I may not be inclined, or able, to go to sleep.

I must find, or devise for myself, ways to allow my mind to rest.

If I *pause*

Now—if I pause

How?—my mind is demanding.

Stop

What?—my mind is asking.

Stop

Pause

Let all the thinking stop

Pause

"*Mind as clear as the open sky*"

*

53

"Nothing is ever found by rushing round a circle . . ."

*

For some, the belief in a deity, omniscient and omnipotent located somewhere in space and time, will be enough.

For some, simply living life here and now, as it seems to be, unconcerned with any idea of immortality or a deity, will be enough.

It is as it should be. It is no one else's business to judge and interfere with the beliefs of another.

If I am mad, that is my business, providing that I do not interfere with, or harm, anyone else.

Each of us is bound to have to live with the consequences of whatever we believe.

But for some of us, there is a possibility, either born out of choosing neither of the two above alternatives, or growing out of choosing either one and then, later, rejecting it: it is the possibility of "entering upon a mystery".

*

Why do I call it a "mystery"?

The root of the word is Greek and means "close lips and eyes". It implies that which cannot be spoken of or seen.

We have suggested that if I speak of or visualize the deity, I am inclined to do so in anthropomorphic terms. It has also been suggested that this is a too simplistic, primitive and literal approach. If the god-idea is far more subtle, it may be that I cannot validly speak of it in worldly terms nor consider it with the logical machinations of the mind.

By "logical machinations" is meant "working it out mentally in either-or terms". The mind is used to finding satisfying answers by this method, certainly, but when it is confronted by a conundrum such as "Which came first, the chicken or the egg?" it cannot choose one way or the other without being wrong!

So, perhaps, in thinking I can make up my mind one way or the other, as to whether there is a deity or not, I am also bound to be wrong?

Maybe I should not try to decide this matter logically?

Although my mind may not care for this—it does like things be logical!—maybe there never has been, nor can there ever be, a *gical* answer to the question and men will go on debating and rguing about it without *ever* proving it one way or the other?

Maybe, by trying to "think about it" in this way—I am missing he point?

*

"*Nothing is ever found by rushing round a circle. Be still. Find ways o become still . . .*"

*

Many of the official representatives of religion, approving of the bove, would then say, "That is why you simply have to have *aith . . .*"

Faith. It is an idea that, clearly, I must consider; but, for now, can certainly say they cannot mean blind self-persuasion, can they, vith the heart ignoring the head?

*

So how can I approach this "mystery"?

*

If I could describe it, it would no longer be a mystery!

Perhaps the most I can say is that, since it will not be describable n worldly terms, then it will not be confined to the physical framework within which I ordinarily think and function. Or, in other words, rather like a dream, it will not be logical, nor will it occur in time (sequence) or space (location).

*

But how will I enter such a mystery?

*

Perhaps by ceasing to assume that I know who I am (believing that I am confined to a physical existence only), and by ceasing to

have beliefs, attitudes and opinions about anything—especiall
myself.

In this way I would consciously be "taken out of myself".

*

And why should I enter such a mystery?

*

May it, possibly, have something to do with resolving th
question: "What is the purpose of my existence?" For must not m
purpose depend upon knowing who I am and must not knowing wh
I am be a mystery and therefore, might not entering that mystery
be the purpose of my existence?

*

How can my mind possibly work out the cause of itself?

*

Yet—through my mind, still comes the question:
What is the purpose of my existence?

Five

What is the purpose of my existence?
Of all the deep questions that I have so far considered this one presents the greatest challenge to me. For the first time there is introduced into the questioning a sense of "activity". Before, the questions were all passive—things happened; I was born; why? I came from somewhere; where? I am; who?

Now, suddenly, there is introduced this sense of "doing"; of *purpose*.

What is the *purpose* of my existence?

Perhaps of all the deep questions this is the one that sends me out in search of like-minded people who may contribute to my quest for an understanding of the "mysteries" of my existence.

Inevitably such a search must include religious systems.

*

The opinion I have of religion, and the value of it in my life, will depend on the experience I have had of religion's official representatives—the priests, bhikkus, rabbis . . .

*

In order to delve into the religious question it is necessary for me to look closely at these people.

What, I wonder, do I make of them?

They wear strange clothes, they officiate in the religious buildings, they intone the prayers and expound the words of the holy scriptures.

They are, they explain, the intermediaries between us and the deity; they are the men of discipline and example; they are the spokesmen of the special dispensations to humanity, as recorded in history or as revealed to them personally.

Or, that is how it appears.

Who *they* think they are is of little importance to me as I approach the threshold of the religious mystery. I judge their presence and performance; according to my understanding, I assess their level of understanding. I decide whether they are self-deluded and talking nonsense or whether they are exceptionally blessed members of society. Accordingly, I will either ignore them and avoid them or I will be attracted to listen to them and maybe seek the benefit of their help, wisdom, or whatever it is that I believe they are capable of providing which I cannot provide for myself.

Perhaps in smaller, more primitive societies, the "holy" man was far more impressive and outstanding in his role. For some reason he was usually recognized and selected for this role early in his life. The "elders" of the tribe were able to read the signs in him, or so it was claimed, and they recognized him as "holy".

What was it that they saw?

Having been recognized for his potential, the chosen one was then groomed during his early years to be the receptacle for the tribe's collective wisdom, as passed on verbally from one generation to the next. Usually this grooming required considerable discipline and sacrifice on the part of the chosen.

Having been so evidently designated, on account of his special gifts and suitability, it is understandable that such a man should come to command the special attention, respect and awe of the other members of the tribe, and even of the leader or chief.

If the chief, either through heredity or particular talents, assumed the responsibility for the conduct of the tribes activities and the maintenance of its laws for security and survival, then it was the "holy" man who, commonly, assumed the role of priest, philosopher, teacher, doctor and psychiatrist—all rolled into one system of knowledge. The "holy" man was concerned with the health of the whole man—physical, mental and spiritual. These three aspects

vere inseparable. Or perhaps it would be truer to say that in such
primitive societies people were not even aware of such a three-fold
division.

But with the increasing complexity of societies, there came
diversity of function. One "holy" man could not hope to cope with
all the demands and developments. In due course the situation
evolved whereby men and women decided that *they wanted* to be
the "holy" ones, i.e., they began to select *themselves* instead of
being chosen by others (although they usually had to—and still do
—submit themselves for examination by a self-selected hierarchy
of established seniors). And such was the proliferation of learning,
that other men and women took on the increasingly specialized
roles of philosophers, teachers, doctors, psychiatrists and social
welfare workers.

*

So—where am *I* in all this?

With a reasonably healthy body and a reasonably functioning
mind, I can get by in the world. But is that enough? Is getting by—
and even possibly doing better than the rest of the herd—all that I
want? Is that as far as my purpose goes?

If it is, fair enough. The teachers will tell me what I want to know
(and what they think I ought to know); the philosophers can
entertain me with interesting ideas; the doctors can sort out my
aches and pains; the psychiatrists can talk me through my problems
if they become troublesome (I can confess all sorts of things without
fear of irksome penance or divine retribution); and the social
workers can provide me with the wherewithal if my daily life gets
in a mess.

What possible need do I have for a "holy" man—who will
probably only speak to me of sin and repentance and perhaps at
the most offer me the charity of the religious establishment?

If that is enough. But—if it isn't? What then? If I find that it
is *not* enough just to get by; if the deep questions continue to nag.
To whom do I turn?

Could it be that if I found the right "holy" man he would know the relationship between the spiritual life, religious practice and everyday living? Perhaps such a man could guide me to an understanding of the deep questions? Perhaps then I would understand the purpose of my life and why it is that the philosophers, teachers, psychiatrists and doctors make their efforts to keep me informed and healthy?

Otherwise, what *is* the point of filling me up with all this learning and then keeping me going for three-score-years-and-ten? There *must* be more to it than just being clever and remaining alive for as long as possible.

*

The official representative of any religion can only command attention, respect and awe to the degree that he is effective in fulfilling his role.

And here, perhaps, there is a paradox. Rather as it is sometimes said that "People get the leaders they deserve," so it could be suggested that "Congregations get the calibre of holy man they deserve." On the other hand, it could equally well be countered, "If the holy man is not inspired within himself, how can he attract the attention and inspire anyone else?"

Again I seem to have come across one of those debatable enigmas for which I suspect there is no conclusive, logical answer one way or the other. Indeed, does it have to be one way or the other? Could it not be that logical mind—which thrives on cause and effect—is not capable of seeing it correctly?

If the mind proves to be incapable—then what is it that brings about spiritual or religious movement in an individual, or a society or a whole race?

Is there "something else"?

*

We might mention here that the noted holy men in history have often only been recognized by a minority in their own time and locality. Furthermore, they have often been rejected by the mass of the people at that time.

It does seem strange that today the vast majority of religious people subscribe to traditions which began centuries ago.

How long, one wonders, will these religions go on for?

Could it be that there could come a time when they will have served their purpose?

Could not man, even now, be evolving into a phase where religions—as we have known them—will no longer be required? Maybe they will pass away as the old-style empires have done? Maybe something else will have to emerge to counteract the world-wide growth of atheistic materialism?

Clearly it will be useless to speculate what this "something" could be.

*

A caterpillar, glancing up at a butterfly darting past, remarked to a neighbouring caterpillar, "You won't catch me going up in one of those!"

*

Maybe we could compromise over this problem of the calibre of the holy man and suggest that the level of understanding of such men will depend on the level of understanding of his followers *and* vice versa.

And I can also see that my estimation of "holiness" in a man will depend on my interpretation and experience of "holiness". If I am looking for reassurance in my beliefs, I will tend to look for the man full of assurance; if I need discipline I will attend the man who is full of discipline and who will give me discipline; if I want to hear the truth, I will listen to the man who seems to know the truth and will tell it to me. Always, of course, it will be reassurrance, discipline and truth in *my* terms.

But that is, surely, reasonable—I can only begin from where I am!

If I approach such a holy man, whatever religion he may belong to, I have taken the first step in the search for understanding of the deep questions within myself. If he understands what I am talking about, then I will listen to him.

*

Now, perhaps I am coming closer to the focus of the religious question.

Without holy men there would be no sacred rites, no one to perform them, no sacred scriptures, no one to read and interpret them, and there would be no places regarded as holy.

I am beginning to realize that in embarking upon the religious quest I am joining a human endeavour which has been going on for thousands of years in many traditions. It does not matter what they called themselves, who they followed, how they expressed themselves—they were all searching, as I am beginning to search, to understand the deep questions within themselves. The self same questions that I am now asking myself.

*

To the extent that I am exploring these matters, am I also seeking to become "holy"? Maybe it is not something that only special people become?

*

I'd better look closer at this idea of "holiness".

Can I be "holy"?

How do I become "holy"—suddenly or gradually?

Or is there something exclusive about a holy man that makes him essentially different from me?

Does he decide that he is holy, or does somebody tell him that he is so—maybe even the deity?

If I am not "holy" now—is it because I lack something, or because I have something "unholy" that must be removed?

I'm sure that it cannot be just a matter of putting on special clothes, making special gestures, reading from the scriptures, remaining celibate, going on fasts—not just a matter of performing the outward show with a solemn face.

Generally speaking, although they differ considerably in style of presentation, I notice certain characteristics in the holy man (or woman). He appears disciplined, confident, and has conviction. These qualities seem to derive from his having sufficient faith in

rtain beliefs, being able, consequently, to sacrifice certain aspects
ordinary life and being able to dedicate himself instead to a
rtain regime.

Now the priest or the bhikku or the rabbi, reading this, will
) doubt reject it out of hand as appallingly simplistic and naive.
Don't you realize," they may say, "how desperately difficult it is
or your 'holy man', as you call him, to maintain his standards of
iscipline and confidence and conviction? We are human too, you
now; subject to all the everyday pressures of humanity. Do you
ippose it is so easy for us to 'keep the faith?' . . ." and so on. And,
f course, they would be right to admonish me; I am being simplis-
c and naive—but perhaps it is for a purpose. After all has been
iid and done, all that really concerns me is: "What is happening
r not happening to *me*, and why?"

How does it come about that another person appears to be "holy"?

Why is it cloaked in such mystery?

If it does not happen to me—if I do not become "holy"—am I
i some way inferior and less privileged?

Does it mean that I cannot be "holy"?

Do I want to be?

As I emerge from my childhood and begin to "become myself",
nd as I face the challenge of taking my place in the world, deciding
vhat I want to be and do, it is possible that I may think of entering
eligion as a "career". However, unless my parents or guardian
nstruct me to (as still happens in some parts of the world), it is
nore likely that I will not choose religion as my full-time occupation.

Does *that* mean that I can never become a holy man or woman?

*

But I am still using the word "holy" without being clear what
I mean by it.

I notice now that the word "holy" seems to be linked—at least
in *sound* even if the purist tells me that it isn't in root—to the word
"whole".

"Whole"—wholesome, complete.

The truly holy man appears to be complete in the sense that he does not seem to desire and pursue the things of the world. Because he is self-sufficient and has put his faith in the deity, he is at peace (providing, that is, he is not trying to influence or interfere in worldly affairs) and does not seem to be anxious and tense in the pursuit of pleasure and the avoidance of pain.

In my observation and contact with holy men and women, I may be over-awed by their titles and trappings. They seem exclusive and I am not always sure how to cope with their being set apart from me and the rest of society. But could it be that I am sensing their strength through commitment? Could it be that it is their self-contained inner strength and their confidence in their deity and their belief that makes them appear complete—and is that not a description of being whole or holy?

The same could apply to a holy place. It also seems self-contained, a sanctuary from the hustle and bustle of the world's concerns and activities, peaceful, and therefore, in not requiring anything of the world, holy.

*

The holy man has self-discipline, confidence and conviction because he has been able to surrender himself—his self-will—to the deity. Whatever his conception of the deity, once he has believed and put his trust in the omnipotence and omniscience of such a deity, his only "one-pointed" endeavour is to devote himself to serving a will superior to his own and constantly attempting to understand what is required of him. To signify his decision to do this, the initiate to holy offices often makes a spoken vow of dedication in the presence of others.

That is one way of looking at it. But I ought not to presume too much. I cannot know exactly how each person experiences his decision to surrender self-will, nor to "what" he has elected to surrender it. The question is—could I do it?

*

That flower is red. Do you agree with me?
Yes, we both say that flower is red.

64

But

How can I ever know for sure that what you are experiencing as "red" is the same as what I am experiencing as "red"?

We both *call* the colour "red"—but neither of us can ever *know* what the other is experiencing.

*

There are so many ways of describing the meaning and experience of holiness—but if I am interested in knowing what it really is, then I will seek to find out and decide for myself.

The fact that a man wears certain vestments, can perform certain rites and quote from the scriptures, is no guarantee that he is what *I* would call holy. Conversely, it may well be that an inconspicuous and reticent man who does not subscribe to any formal religion may well be the most holy man I have ever met.

I, myself, may find that I am overcome by the sight of a magnificent sunset, by a glorious flower, by waves crashing against rocks, by a beautiful animal; I may find myself "transported" by the sound of bird-song, of the wind among trees, of a human voice; by the scent of the early morning, by a gentle touch . . . In those moments, do I not surrender myself? Are they not holy in that they are whole, complete, with nothing lacking? And do I not marvel and feel my heart "going out"?

Momentarily, am I not made whole?

*

How am I made whole?

If it is to do with becoming complete, and that means not lacking anything, then I must examine what I think I lack. Possibly then, to the extent that I can begin to eliminate the pursuit of those things that I think I want but find I do not really need, I am nearer to being whole?

If I think in terms of being made whole rather than becoming holier, I can perhaps avoid the problem of pride. For, if I begin to succeed in my quest, I may begin to think that I am "holier than thou".

C
65

But in no way can I be "wholer than thou".

*

Through my early contact with the formality of religion, I a
likely to have been affected, possibly even awed, by its mystique.

Could it be that the outer form of religion—the ritual and th
pomp, the titles and the hierarchies—has diverted my attentio
from the fact that such outer show is just a performance?

Could there be, underlying this show, an inner message to guid
me in my religious quest?

Could it be that behind the outer appearance there are teaching
that are meant to show me what fulfilment as an individual woul
mean—how I may become "holy"?

*

Until the present century, every state accepted religion as a
intrinsic part of the life of its people. To varying degrees th
religious ingredient was championed, encouraged and valued. Wit
the growth of science, industry and learning, with the growin
emphasis on material wealth, this century has seen a decline i
recognition of the religious establishment, and even active elimina
tion of it in some parts of the world.

Religion has tended to become an irrelevant hang-over from th
past—or, at least, that is the case for the majority of peoples; it ha
become something at the best tolerated for the sake of the few, bu
no longer a vital centre around which a given society revolves.

But—could it be that, as we see the emergence of the power
of the atheistic state, we might also be witness to the "resurrection"
of vital religious teachings?

This is not a vain assumption; for at some moment in the dim
mest, most distant past of our evolution, pressures of life force
the emergence of an alternative direction into the minds of men
religion emerged out of *need*. Can we not, today, see chaos all aroun
us; does not that chaos bring to the fore of our minds a crying nee
—are not many of us now looking, each in his own way, for "something to believe in", for a new religion?

66

Perhaps it is as if the vital "seeds" sown centuries ago have now finished their growing and that, as the flowering of faith-religions made, so we might see the first fruits of an evolving "spirituality"?

Just as the primitive "seed" religions of the nature-gods were an everyday fact of life for early man so now—but a quantum jump in understanding compared to those ages—could we see the inner spiritual inspiration becoming that everyday fact of life for increasing numbers of individuals on a world-wide scale?

*

It is interesting for me to note here how my mind works. Its first, immediate reaction to the suggestion of a present spiritual evolvement in man is to reject it out of hand.

"Quite the contrary," it says, "Man is going downhill. Look at the chaos, the self-inflicted misery and suffering in the world today. How can anyone suggest that this is a growth of spirituality . . ."

But what mind cannot see is that, if there is a spiritual evolution going on, then—*mind will also be evolving.*

Does the caterpillar know that it will one day be a butterfly?

Does the caterpillar consider the chrysalis that it is to become? If so, does it see the chrysalis as a step in its evolution—or, as death? And is not the chrysalis state *both*? For, as much as it is the death of the caterpillar, it is also its evolutionary state.

Does the chrysalis *know* anything?

Before the emergence of the butterfly, the chrysalis progresses from a dormant, waiting state into a state of great activity. It twitches and pulls to such an extent that it tears itself apart. Only then can the butterfly, the culmination of the cycle, emerge for its brief, glorious reign as a creature of the air and a creator in the chain of life.

Could it not, perhaps, be the same with mind? If it is to emerge in a new state, suffused with spirituality from "above" and freed from the self-absorption from "below"—it cannot *know* its new form until it has gained that state.

*

Let me take it a step further.

It could be that mankind itself is emerging from its "childhood" and is starting to become independent, reasoning its way out o superstition and make-believe, starting to become "its true self" So, at the same time that there is an espousal to materialism in on part of itself, so its "higher" nature is stimulated in another par It also may be seen to be tearing itself apart.

*

What is really going on as we look back over the ages and con template the situation of today is a mystery.

From time to time, philosophers devise new explanations fo the situation as they find it in their lifetimes.

I do not know what moves me, but, as I play the part, I dul try to explain and justify it, especially to myself.

It seems that the more disenchanted I become with the situatio in which I find myself, the more I will endeavour to change it.

The more I find dissatisfaction with my old explanations fo what is going on, the more fervently will I look for new ones.

The more that I feel that I have not been told the truth, th stronger will be the desire to find it for myself.

Rotting compost is a powerful aid to new growth.

Simultaneously with the feeling that just getting by and muddlin on as I am is not enough, so I begin to hear the deep question stirring: "Who am I?" "Where did I come from?" "Why was born?" "What is the purpose of my existence?"

*

'Nothing is ever found by rushing round a circle. Be still. Find way to become still. Then listen, at the centre, to the questions of you heart. For it is these many questions which will lead you to the few strong vital questions which will lead you to your Spirit. Trust th questions. They are all that you need. Do not be contented with th many answers the world will offer. Listen to the Questions . . . B still, listen . . ."

*

If the questions stir me from my apathy or interrupt my head-
ong race of activity and pursuit of desires, then they demand my
ttention.

And of all the questions that checks me as I contemplate the
ort of life I am leading, perhaps the most poignant is:

"What happens when I die?"

*

One of the marks of a truly holy man is that he does not fear
death because he knows what it means.

Understanding death implies a knowing of who or what dies.

What dies?

Who dies?

It is said that life is a preparation for death. Is death, then, the
ultimate completion?

Perhaps being holy in life means an understanding of becoming
whole in death?

For what could be a more complete culmination to this life than
immortality?

*

Do I die?

What happens when I die?

Six

What happens when I die?

If it is at all true, as was stated in the last chapter, that the holy man does not fear death because he knows what it means—then here must be the most compelling bait to draw a questioning/questing person towards the religious phenomenon.

As has already been observed, death appears as the incomprehensible full-stop to "life"; for it is very rare that we consider "life" as a preparation for "death".

If, therefore, we get a hint that there are certain people in the world who can expound the mystery of death, are we not bound to seek them out, in the hope that they may *enlighten* us?

It is the question of death—"What happens when I die?" or, more subtly and perhaps more precisely, "Do *I* die?"—that is the religious devotee's trump card.

For they speak about "the here-after", "the after-life", "the enlightened ones", "fully realized persons" and so on . . .

Such hints that there is further knowledge available to me, that could lead to an understanding of the enigma of death, draws me towards the religious question.

*

Let us make no mistake about it.

In one aspect, the question of religion is something I can easily put aside. I can, and will, carry on without it whilst my life is full of absorbing, exciting and exacting activities—and most especially

70

if I am already acquainted with formal religion and it does not attract me. I can, quite simply, get on with the challenges and pleasures of daily living without giving religion a thought—until the day dawns, as I accept that it inevitably will, when death puts an end to my thinking and doing.

In the other aspect, according to my nature and according to the state of the world about me and how it affects me, I may not be able to ignore religion—at least, not indefinitely.

If the deep questions become important to me, I have no choice but to face them. And, once I truly enter upon their exploration, I will find that I am entering a labyrinth—the mysterious labyrinth of my mind.

Will religion, in the widest meaning of the word, guide me in this exploration?

*

As I begin to wake up from my "dream" life, that make-believe world which I have accepted as the reality, I enter strange and unfamiliar territory. I step on to a path which leads into the labyrinth of my *mind* as I seek to discover what the reality of my existence really is.

It can begin like this: "Why do I think what I am thinking?" —and the first step has been taken into the twisting maze of the labyrinth . . .

*

"I have hidden it," he replied, "I have hidden it in the one place that Man will never think of looking for it."
"But, where is that?" demanded the others.
"I have hidden it," said the old god, "within Man himself."

*

Who enters my mind and observes what is going on there?
Surely, no other person can—only I?
What is the mind?
Why should I enter and explore it?

71

Because I have to live with it? Because I have to put up with what it thinks?

Because, no matter where I go—even to the far corners of the earth, and no matter what I do—even if I devise all manner of "escape", whilst I am alive and conscious, I have to live with myself?

*

How can I possibly truly love any one or any thing—if I am ignorant and dissatisfied with myself?

How can I hope to know another person—if I do not know who I am, if I do not know myself?

*

On the *face* of it, religion is just another performance. Going to the holy place is just like going to the theatre, or going to the dentist, or shopping. It is something I may do from time to time. If it satisfies some appetite or requirement in me, then it will make me feel good and comforted and dutiful, or whatever.

I can leave it at that. So be it.

Or I can enter more deeply into the whole religious question. That may not necessarily mean going to the holy place more often. But it may mean that the religious question grows in intensity and begins to penetrate and inform more and more of the things I do and why I do them.

I begin to see that it is no light matter. It is not like taking up just another hobby.

It is extremely serious—though that does not mean that it need be solemn and humourless.

In its widest and deepest meaning, the religious question can become the focus of my *whole* life.

*

If I put these two aspects together—what is going on in my mind and how the religious question affects my thinking and what

I believe—then I may see that, *essentially*, religion has a great deal to do with disciplining my mind—or rather, what goes on in it.

*

What is the mind?

"Mind" is a word that I will have learned to use early in my life. I vaguely know what I mean by it, but, have I ever really considered it?

As far as locating my mind is concerned, it seems to be inside my head. I have learned that, whatever mind is, it is closely associated with my brain—that spongy, greyish, intricate mass of tissue containing millions of cells. By means of an electro-chemical exchange of "energy-particles", countless "messages" are transmitted and stored or dissipated within a complex nerve network. It apparently functions something like a very sophisticated computer, assimilating and disseminating information and instruction. At least, that is the sort of model that serves the scientific point of view . . . It is a kind of explanation.

Further evidence for the brain being the site of my mind is provided by scientific experiment, medicine and other external factors that undeniably affect the brain (for example, an accident) all of which demonstrate that chemicals and other physical interference can change the personality and thinking of the creature. In a state of shock, such as concussion, a person can move about but is not conscious of what he is doing and "is not there" in his thinking.

All such evidence adds to the idea of my mind being in my head.

Much ingenious investigation of the brain has been carried out by scientists, and "maps" of it show which parts of it, particularly the cortex, are concerned with different activity—for example, which areas deal with seeing, smelling and speaking.

BUT—and it is a huge "but"—no one can tell me *how* the brain cells convert the so-called electro-chemical exchanges into what you and I *experience* as a particular sight, smell or sound.

Does the knowledge that my mind is a highly complex machine

for information assimilation and dissemination have the remotest connection with my experience and with me myself?

*

This has enormous implications, and is what we might call another quantum jump, from a mechanical scientific explanation to the mystery of the experience itself.

Even at what might be called the simplest level, it is an utter mystery how sensory impressions—which give me the sense of my being *in* the world—are connected and are converted to my experience *of* the world.

All the scientific explanations have a certain application—hence their strength and attraction—in dealing with disease, illness and other physical malfunctions; in constructing all manner of tools and devices that I can use in my everyday physical existence. There is a whole, vast panorama of human learning and invention here— and very impressive it is. But it could be seen as totally superficial in that it is all concerned only with easing, maintaining, and prolonging the life of my body, the society in which I live and, to a certain extent, the rest of mankind.

It seems as if the whole of human effort is devoted to living as long and as pleasurably as possible. But for what purpose should I want to hang on for another ten, twenty or thirty years, no matter how pain-free and pleasantly?

If I penetrate a little deeper, I am confronted with utter mystery. What I have learned and what I am persuaded I am living for seems a gigantic confidence trick! For I cannot answer the question; what on earth am I really here for?

At a certain level of functioning—survival—man is exceedingly clever and explains many things away. But if I scratch that sophisticated surface, what do I find? That he is utterly ignorant, self-deluded and naive? Could it be that, for all his extraordinary ingenuity and inventiveness, man has at the same time indulged in the most amazing, self-deceptive foolishness?

*

How does my body know how to work?

How does it know how to heal a wound, grow a hair, how to breathe?

Can I, if I so wish, grow a third arm, see what is not there, create a god?

How does an idea enter my mind. Where does it come from?

Can I make yesterday come again tomorrow, put a star in my pocket, walk on water?

How does a plant know how to grow a flower?

If I say "I cooked a meal", did I actually *cook* it? Or did heat cook it?

*

And if it is impossible to know how a sense impression is converted into a sensory experience, how much "more" impossible must it be to know what thoughts, memories, ideas and beliefs actually *are*?

*

In the early days of my learning, I may be told that what I am looking at is "a table". From then onwards, since everyone else calls similar objects "tables", I believe that that is what it is.

But "table" is only a name for it. It is what it is *called*. Is that what it really *is*?

If someone from another country, speaking a different language, calls it by a different name, does it change into something else?

What *is* it before I learn to call it a table?

*

I readily accept all sorts of names for physical objects and this enables me to take my place in the world and communicate with others who "speak the same language". Fortunately, other people around me know what I mean when I say "bread", "water", "clothes", "house" and so on. To be able to communicate and trade in such a language enables me to survive as a body.

But the situation becomes far more difficult when I wish to communicate the abstract.

How well, for example, can I tell someone the nature and intensity of my feelings and emotions? I cannot say with any hope of being understood that my happiness is "six metres long" or my anger is "three kilograms heavy" or that the heat of my desire is "one hundred degrees centigrade"!

So how can I accurately describe to someone what I mean by "faith", "consciousness", "love" or "god"?

*

I say that I have a mind and that I associate it with my brain. But can I say what it *is*?

How big is it? How heavy is it?

Where is it when I am unconscious or "absent-minded" or dead?

We speak of people as being "mindless" or "mindful" or "out of their mind"; but what *on earth* do we mean?

*

Although I can say that certain things go on in my mind—thinking, believing, memorizing, visualizing, imagining, reasoning and so on—I have no real knowledge of what these things *are*, nor how they come to be there.

And if my heart "goes out"—if I yearn, desire, am in anguish, love, idolize, worship—do I know what I am expressing?

To be sure, I am entering a labyrinth.

*

"Where are you going?" he asked.

"Into the labyrinth," I replied.

"Is that wise?"

"It is inevitable—I must discover what is at its centre. I must see it for myself."

"Then, remember," he said, "you will have to find your own way back."

"What do I require for the journey?" I enquired.

"Clear vision and a loving heart."

"How can I acquire such qualities?"

"They are already yours. You have simply to remember."
"How can I remember?"
"By listening—from the still centre of your being."
Be still. Find ways to become still . . .
Listen to the Questions and follow them; they are your open sesame . . .

*

At face value in my estimation, I can accept religion as something that I need—as I need to eat, to sleep and to drink; or I can reject it—as I may reject smoking, or alcohol, or thieving, or lying.

In other words, I can take it or I can leave it.

If I take to religion, it will be in response to my needing, intellectually or emotionally, the god-idea, the holy man and the holy place—to support some identified or unidentified desire or lack in me.

At a "deeper" level, when I enter the labyrinth of my mind, I will want to know what goes on in the mind, what religion is, why the mind needs religion, how (if *I* am to be made whole) the mind can understand what is going on—and, thus, what the deep questions are telling the mind about its limitations, its functions, to what it must be obedient for its peace, and how it can fulfil itself.

*

Maybe, if the mind cannot believe that there is a god, I can "believe *in* God . . . Allah . . . Brahman . . . Jehovah . . ."

*

As the body grows, the mind begins to receive and absorb all kinds of information through the senses. Not all the continual bombardment of impressions can be "recognized", so the mind selects only a certain amount—those which, for some reason, interest it.

Broadly speaking, the mind selects, interprets and reacts to the environment in accordance with certain priorities and requirements. If something dangerous or threatening approaches, the mind alerts

77

defensive mechanisms even before I am aware that it has done so. Routine responses, such as moving the body about to ease discomfort, are dealt with by mind without my noticing. Other parts of the mind get on with regulating body temperature, breathing, blood circulation and numerous other functions entirely without "me" knowing anything about them except when they go wrong. If a problem arises, another part of the mind sets about working out a solution. If a desire arises, the mind processes the factors which will enable or prevent fulfilment of that desire.

If I was to set down all the varied activities and functions of the mind I could fill pages, and still find that I had left as many more out of my list.

But I use the word "mind" to cover an enormous range of activities of widely differing kinds—and I rarely pause to look at the nature of the organs of their functions, many of which *I* am unaware of.

So, who am I who lays claim to this mind which does so much that I do not know about?

*

What must interest me for the moment is that, apart from the individual characteristics, it is what the mind selects and processes according to its own particular nature (and how does it acquire its individual nature?) that leads to my thinking being "me" as distinct from anyone else. According to what my mind tends to select, I can be said to have particular predispositions, predilections, prejudices and so on. According to how my mind processes the material it receives, I can be said to think in a certain way.

We say, "Oh, that's what he would say . . ." or "That's how he would see it . . ."

As the result of this mind selecting and processing, which is peculiar in its ingredients and permutations to "this person", the person acts in a certain way and speaks in a certain way in response to stimuli in varying situations. The person is said to have a certain personality. Along with his particular physical characteristics and the particular name by which he is called, this personality is recog-

78

nized by others as being a particular person. It is the combination of these factors which give rise to this particular "me".

As a result of exchange with the environment, there is created an immediate experience of "becoming and being myself". It may appear to have been formed arbitrarily and accidentally, but for whatever reason, this is me, here and now.

*

Tomorrow you might meet a slightly different me.

For the me of yesterday is not quite the me of today.

Here is the problem for me; to seem constant and consistent enough to be able to hang on to the belief that me is an integrated entity and not just a random and uncontrolled collection of bits and pieces, frequently threatening to disintegrate because one bit disagrees with another bit.

It is important to seem whole.

*

The "me", my particular personality—which from here onwards might be recognized as the ego—is an inconstant creation, being influenced and affected by whatever happens to it from moment to moment, depending for its maintenance on a continual interchange with the environment.

When the mind sleeps or is otherwise unconscious, it disappears, at least so far as *I* am concerned.

So also, when the mind is passive, quiet, empty, at rest—it is as if the ego disappears. As soon as activity resumes, the ego reassembles.

*

Of course, all that I have attempted to say above is only a crude and simplistic description of what is evidently, when you look at it, a very complex process.

However, if you pause to observe, then maybe you will agree that it is more or less what seems to happen.

And if you don't agree—then, perhaps you will agree that you don't know precisely what goes on, any more than I do.

You may even ask why it is so important to understand the nature of the mind and the ego? Ought we not to leave well alone? Are we not complicating matters; trying to comprehend the incomprehensible?

But in the context of this book, it is a crucial factor in our approach to the religious question. (Of course, there are other approaches—but you are reading *this* book!)

In fact, I would go further and say that it is *the* most crucial factor in understanding all religious traditions; because the moulding, discipline and disposition of the mind—and hence the state of the ego at any moment—is crucial to being religious.

*

Most of the time, the ego acts and reacts automatically to what goes on. Time passes and I am unconscious of it. Where was I? It is as if I am asleep and the ego gets on with it all—pursuing pleasure, avoiding pain, successfully or unsuccessfully, according to the efficiency of the mind—and doing it all *in my name*!

Then, suddenly, I wake up to "being here". I wake up to what is being said, done, dreamed, imagined, by my mind and my body! It is as if there is a stepping into another dimension—what some religious systems call a "rise in consciousness". Suddenly instead of being lost in the mind's concerns, or whatever else it is that I have been, I am awake, here, *now*, to what is going on.

Because I can witness what has been going on in my mind, I am not my mind. I could not even speak of "my" mind unless there was an acknowledgement that it belonged to someone.

Who am I who enters this mind, gets lost in it, comes out of it? Who is it who enters the labyrinth of the mind?

*

Now I must be most careful how I express myself.

I—whoever I am—have a body that I call my body. I have a name, my name. I have a mind, my mind.

So who am I who says that I possess them?

My body changes with age, my mind changes (or rather, its

contents and the processing change); but *I* am that unchanging one who has looked out through the eyes of the child in the photograph and who is looking now at this page, this writing, this hand.

And *you*, you are looking through your eyes at these words and your mind is processing them. Each word, as you read it—now— each word is being read through your eyes and processed by your mind—now—and again . . .

now

But—who are you? When you turn over this page and read further and time has passed, will it be the same you who is doing the looking? Your eyes will be older, your mind will have worked a little more, but will the *I* in you have worked any more or grown any older? What is working? What is growing older?

*

"When you enter the labyrinth, *remember*, you must find your own way back . . ."

*

The essence of the religious question is understanding that the real *I* is distinguishable from the ego—that changing, utilitarian, multi-faceted, temporal personality that is *me*.

*

Why is it the essence of the religious question?

"*Once upon a time, when the world was fresh and green and young, Man . . .*"

Once upon *what* time?

"*He had been told that he had been created immortal, that the gods held his Spirit for him . . .*"

His *Spirit*?

"*. . . and he would take his place amongst them and be a god as they were . . .*"

What does it all *mean*? That is the religious question.

*

The real *I* is distinguishable from the ego, from *me*.

It is the essence of the religious question because the ego, on the basis of the mind's experience of the world, will never be able to prove the validity of the god-idea, never be able to decide convincingly whether there is a god "out there" or not.

The mind will never be able to work out the cause of itself.

A shadow might just as well try to prove whether there is a sun or not.

Mind will never be able to work out who it is that it belongs to, as if that someone were separate from itself. Despite all its explanations of the mechanism of the universe, it will never be able to answer, in its own terms, the question—"Why this universe?"

The mind will never be able to provide other than partial explanations in answer to the deep questions.

But on the other hand, could it be that my mind could *understand* who I—the one asking the questions—am?

Rather as if the shadow simply acknowledged that the sun was the cause of itself, and that when the sun was not there . . . it was not there?

*

Mind will never be able to answer the deep questions that stir *in it*—and yet, they are there; troubling it, puzzling it.

Why this universe? How was it created? What is it for?

Seven

Why this universe? How was it created? What is it for?
How can a particular mind, with its inevitably partial and
arbitrarily collected learning, ever hope to answer such absolute
questions as these?

What can such a mind ever hope to devise but feeble explanations
in its own limited terms?

To expect more of it would be as if to expect my shadow to say
to me, "Why are you standing between me and the sun?"

*

We are now looking into the very depths of our understanding
and the experience is unfamiliar and confusing, mainly because we
do not know who is looking at what, and whatever descriptions and
explanations the mind comes up with can never be more than
superficial. The vocabulary we have learned from the world seems
inadequate and the mind becomes bewildered in trying to work out
intellectually who I am, what is me, where I or me came from, who
or what dies and so on.

It is indeed a mysterious labyrinth.

But, if we are moved to do so, entering such a labyrinth can
become an absorbing and rewarding journey. Many people are
engaged in the search for the centre of it in themselves and each of
them, it seems, chooses a particular path. They each take their *own*
wrong-turnings, meet their *own* cul-de-sacs, make their *own*
progress (even if that means not knowing how far they have yet to

go but knowing only how far they have so far travelled) along their *own* particular path.

Those who do not choose to enter the labyrinth remain vulnerable and mortal, inexorably the victims of the world's circumstances.

There could not be enough space in this book, nor in a thousand such books, to consider all the aspects of this search. In any case reading about it is only a preparation.

Only I can enter my path in my experience.

Only *you* can enter *your* path in *your* experience—just when *you* decide to do so.

*

Already, in the above paragraphs, we have taken a vital step. For we have had a taste of *how* the journey in the labyrinth of mind may be taken, and, more importantly, *expressed*.

If it is not expressed, does the journey exist for us? If it is not expressed, do we know that we are "on a journey"? And, if we do not "know" we are on a journey—then can we be possibly going anywhere?

The man who wakes up one morning believing that he is "god" without knowing how he acquired the belief, is in danger of being thought "mad" by others and possibly also by himself.

If, however, he had a language with which to express his journey to this state of "godliness", he might be seen to be sane indeed.

This language is *simile*—the art of expressing through the likening of one thing to another.

My mind and your mind cannot know or speak of the confusing complexities of its own nature, but we can recognize the physical confusions of entering into a maze or a labyrinth. So, by speaking in physical terms of being lost in a labyrinth (or maze), with its cul-de-sacs, its wrong-turnings and its baffling alley-ways, we are each expressing the *subtle* experiences of the labyrinth of mind that that individual mind cannot express or know for itself.

As we continue on this quest, we will find that all the religious traditions adopt this device.

Indeed, we already use it for ourselves. It is our way of expressing

84

or ourself, in physical terms, the mysteries of the unmanifest experience.

*

All religious traditions are combinations of guides, instructions, encouragements and warnings—about approaching the religious question and for living a religious life.

Each, in its own way of describing it, exhorts the aspirant to have faith.

This can mean that in order to enter the mystery of *myself*, I will no longer be able to rely on my learning, my partial explanations, my beliefs and my assumptions. It is as if I have to abandon the security of what I think I know and can work out for myself, and must put my trust in an "open mind", trusting in nothing "out there".

Some people, discontent with the limitations of getting by in the world, approach the labyrinth because their hearts desire the truth and real meaning. Others, with the same discontent, approach formal religion as simply something they can surrender themselves to—thereby surrendering responsibility for themselves.

However, whatever the reason for the approach, what is being looked for is discipline and guidance—*for the mind*.

*

The mind is ordinarily very busy.

To a large extent, its traffic of information and instruction goes on unnoticed, especially where movement and regulation of the body are concerned.

Sometimes the mind processes are idling in dreams, sometimes they are being "entertained", sometimes they are learning and processing information, having conversations, imagining, working out problems and plans . . .

There is all manner of activity, which we, collectively, call "thinking".

And then—suddenly—into this relatively gentle thinking process, emotions erupt.

85

Stimulated either by outside impressions coming through th
senses, or internally by evocative thinking ("simile thinking")–
suddenly—there are desires or fears, firing or freezing, dominatin
the mind and causing all manner of confusion. The mind tries har
to cope with such disruptions and obediently attempts to work ou
how to acquire that which is desired or to avoid that which is feared
Sometimes only little things are involved and they are soon resolved
But sometimes, dealing with the desires or fears—especially whe
they are deeply seated and strong—can become a battle-royal
going on and on, particularly when the desire is not fully satisfie
or the fear not totally resolved—culminating in frustration on th
one hand and a continual state of worry on the other.

Both these situations produce the background tension to life
causing blockages of energy that can explode in anger and violenc
or causing a continual draining away of vital energy that results ir
tiredness and even illness.

Clearly, I have no control over when such desires and fears ar
going to invade my mind. But do I have control once they hav
done so?

How does the mind respond?

Is it able to cope with them or not?

Do I not, sometimes, do foolish and irrational things as a resul
of this apparent bombardment?

*

How, I wonder, do I judge how irrational and foolish my
behaviour is?

I must have some set standards from which I believe that I am
deviating.

What is normal and where do the restraints come from?

Do the restraints come from my mind having been conditioned
and educated as to what is normal and lawful according to family,
society and the state or religion to which I belong?

Or can such restraint come from having an innate, instinctive
knowledge of what is reasonable, natural and dignified?

And if there *is* an innate knowledge and it is apparently in

86

conflict with the conditioned knowledge ... which of the two possible paths of the labyrinth do I take?

Whatever the answers to such questions—and undoubtedly there would be considerable debate and difference of opinion—the fact is that mind often becomes baffled in dealing with such a situation and with the many conflicting voices, both inner and outer, which try to resolve the problem.

Different parts of mind produce different answers, sometimes contradictory. One part wants to act one way, another part wants to do the opposite. Having acted—whether a clear decision was made or not—another part of mind may later regret, have misgivings, countermand, seek redress, cover up, or, certainly, criticize.

Where does all this get me?

The mind seems unreliable, inconsistent, inefficient, as it is thrown this way and that by any desire or fear that takes possession of it.

But don't let's be too hard on it! That same mind always tries to restore the balance, so that "me" can seem an integrated and sensible person!

If, however, it fails to do so, then all manner of mental disorders can resolve the desperation.

*

If the mind is full of activity, and memory is short-lived, the deeper inconsistencies and contradictions may not be noticed. They can, after all, simply be explained away as being just part of my personality or character. But the continual effort to behave reasonably within the accepted norms of my surroundings is rarely comfortable or peaceful (thus my desire to be entertained and "taken out of myself"). For, the strong desires and fears have exceedingly deep roots in my being.

Desire has to do with seeking satisfaction, fulfilment, peace, happiness and perfection—in fact, union with that which will make me complete and whole. Even what the world calls "the selfish desires"—if we look at them closely, we may see that they too have,

87

in essence, this same quality. How can a man behave "selfishly". What is it—to be selfish? What is the point of it?

At its best, is not "to be selfish" a desire to be unified with the true self—the *I* in *me*?

And, at its worst, is not "to be selfish" to desire for *me* a more peaceful, unified experience of that same self? It is only in what we *think* will bring about such unity and peace that the discrepancies arise. If I take something that belongs to someone else, for example it is because I desire it for *me*—but in taking it for *myself* I have simply failed to see that I am denying it to the *self* from which I took it. What has been missed by *me* is the fact that only something *I* truly own will give *me* the satisfaction, fulfilment, peace, happiness, and perfection that *I* am seeking. Only then can *I* be whole.

As the deep questions emerge and there is consciousness of becoming and being me, there is an awareness of all the difficulties— dissatisfaction, unfulfilment, unhappiness, isolation, loneliness, incompleteness and imperfection. The creative sex energy that fires my being produces all kinds of objects and images that become my goals and ideals—all those ambitions and achievements which will bring the perfection and fulfilment of my life. That same sex energy, in its negative, frustrating, aspect, brings with it bitter emotions such as jealousy, lust, envy and covetousness.

But in its widest aspect—on the grand human physical scale— this firing, testing, consuming energy has to do with selection and survival of the strongest and with preservation of the species.

Inextricably interwoven with the creative (or destructive) desire is the fear which is basically to do with the individual's desire to avoid pain and death. From the ego's point of view, it is translated into the defence of my identity, my territory, my possessions—for, if I lose any of these then where am I?

In its deepest aspect, on the scale of a particular human being, this fear has to do with self-survival.

*

The mind is constantly beset with the problems of how to procure this and avoid that, and how best to cope with the eruptions of motion. According to conditioning and learning, and adopted patterns of habitual response, "me" thinks and does all sorts of things "in character" and "out of character".

We must, surely, all observe ourselves saying and doing these things?

Sometimes I am pleased with myself, sometimes displeased. Sometimes I say, "That's not like me . . ." or "That's just the sort of thing I would do . . ." Sometimes I say, "I wish I was like so-and-so . . ." and at other times I will say, "I'm glad I'm not like so-and-so . . ."

All this time I am judging how I want to appear to myself and to other people; and I am constantly trying to maintain an image of being consistent and self-contained.

Now, in all this to-ing and fro-ing—do I exercise free will? By whose will am I doing what I do? Do I really have a choice? Is the sum total of all these make-do reactions really me?

If I am pushed and pulled by all sorts of accidental happenings, can there ever be a constant and real me? Amidst all this consternation, can I ever be "whole"?

*

Religious traditions provide rules of conduct and the keys to resolving the conflicts and tribulations of the mind.

They provide a discipline and guidance for the mind and consequently for me. And since how I act is dependent on instructions from my mind, religion also disciplines and guides my behaviour in the world.

If I adopt a particular religion, it will provide me with a "rule book" as to what I may or may not say and do; what I ought and ought not to say and do.

In relation to how I think and act, the rules of conduct will concern how I treat my body and how I treat all other living creatures—the world and all things in it, whether friendly or hostile.

Broadly speaking, the rules always call for consideration, compassion, gentleness and forgiveness. In all my behaviour there should be a moderation; there should be no excess of those things that are not expressly forbidden; and there should be strict avoidance of the forbidden things.

I am asked to curb and eliminate all manner of exploitation, aggression and greed; and all wilful acts which derive from my selfish desire, depriving others for the sake of gaining for myself.

Religious traditions are concerned to promote what in their view is the most seemly attitude and conduct required to deal with roused emotions, especially as manifesting in sexual urges and sensual appetites. They offer guidance as to how such energy should be expressed, channelled, suppressed or transformed.

They are concerned to establish constructive and useful attitudes towards work, especially in the directing of it towards the benefit and service of others.

They seek to encourage the natural kindness of the heart to find expression in charitable deeds . . .

They often indicate those institutions in society—government, law, medicine, for example—which should be respected, obeyed and honoured . . .

They frequently enumerate the pursuits and habits which should be abjured for the harm they will do to mind and body. And here, they not only refer to the pursuits applying to carnal appetites and practice but also to destructive *thinking* . . .

*

Each of the religious traditions has long lists of do's and don'ts, of rights and wrongs, of commandments and laws . . .

Many of them are reasonable and obvious, but others are obscure. Most of them we learn so early and so well that they become a part of our individual personality and we see them as our own and not as acquired.

Very often they are not questioned by us. Until, one day, we may ask:

Where does the *authority* come from for these rules?

*

Amongst the scriptures of the world is a vast catalogue of rights and wrongs which, if simply accepted as god-given, will enable my mind to decide more easily and allow me to behave more consistently. It may give me greater peace of mind, and it will certainly lessen the chances of my being a disruptive element in society.

The incentive is straightforward. If I disobey, I will have committed wrong, will feel guilty, will be judged, and will either be forgiven or punished in some way or other. The restraint is maintained through fear, especially in my early years, for it is fear of consequences that most effectively influences my behaviour.

However, such is the subtle nature of desire, I am also influenced by the fact that good conduct will bring reward. If the ultimate reward is to be some privileged status in this or a further life, then that future reward is worth some sacrifice now.

It will only be later, beyond the web of desire and fear, that I will be able to consider what it may mean to act for the love of my fellow men and the deity.

(This last statement I can see will be debatable—but, again, I must be as honest as is possible. Are there not many times when I say I am acting for the love of my fellow men—when, in fact, my action is really to gratify some desire or avoid some fear in myself. Do I not take up "causes" because it gratifies my ego, "me", to belong to such causes? Or, if I subscribe to the god-idea, do I not obey some religious rule simply because I am afraid of what may happen if I do not obey it? And is not this very close to "superstitious behaviour"?)

*

In addition, I am further insured. No matter how disciplined, dedicated, and "good" I am, I may still fall the victim of misfortune; but if I have believed, I can rely on the comfort and strength of the deity to sustain me. I may even accept that, because my misfortune is not the result of my wilfulness and sin (as far as I can see), then it is the will of the deity for reasons unknown to me, either as a challenge to my faith or to fulfil the deity's purpose for me.

*

Such is one way of looking at the role of religion.

If, in my adoption of a particular religious tradition, my reason, conscience, intuition and instinctive "feelings" (whatever all those functions *are*) are not offended, well and good. I will have learned to surrender to the deity and I will have learned how to conduct myself in the world. I will, in short, be able to say "I am holy".

But—am I *wholly* holy?

*

Does this view of religion cater for the deep questions?

There is still "Who am I?" "Where did I come from?" "Why was I born?" "What happens when I die?" "Do I die?" "What is the purpose of my existence?"

Is it enough to be a disciplined human being?

*

Certainly it is—if that is all *I* am.

If *I am* a human being—no thing more nor less than that—then it is enough that *I* should be disciplined.

But, through the exploration of this book we have suggested that *I* may be more than just this body; more, even, than just this mind.

Let *me* try an experiment.

But—first—let us look at the peculiar nature of "a book":

If it is written, "Let *me* try an experiment"—and if you (the reader) read, "Let *me* try an experiment" . . . then are not the writer and the reader both *me*?

Perhaps a more correct expression would be—"Let *us* try an experiment?"

I hold my right hand out in front of *me*.

I am looking at my right hand.

Who is doing the looking?

I am?

Who am I who is doing the looking?

Me?

What is seeing?

How is the seeing being done?

If *I* am doing the seeing—and what is seen belongs to that *I* . . . how is it that *I* am able to look at a part of *I*?

No, no—*I* am looking at *me*.

So . . . who am *I* who is doing the looking?

I am still looking at the right hand . . .

What is this hand?

Whose hand is it?

Mine?

Is it? I don't know much about it.

Do *I* own the hand—or, does the hand belong to *me*?

*

Beyond or beneath the religious requirements of the ego—of *me*—is the religious *mystery*. (Mystery—"close lips or eyes"—that which cannot be spoken of or seen . . .)

Beyond or beneath the performance of formal religion maybe there is an indication of this mystery?

As we look into the religious traditions, and all the teachings and stories (the similes) essential to them, we will find much that is illogical and inexplicable to the ordinary scope of the mind functions. For example, events are related which are miraculous and magical, and holy men are reported as saying things which seem little more than nonsensical riddles; they are quite outside my common experience as far as the ordinary events and conversations of my everyday life are concerned.

What can they mean?

Have I pushed them aside as being inexplicable and because they seem to have no relevance as I get on with the everyday demands and pursuits of living? Maybe I have simply put such things down to belonging to times when men were more superstitious and gullible, ignorant and less advanced scientifically?

Have I, perhaps, been missing something significant by simply taking these things at their face value and then dismissing them?

Perhaps if I was a little less involved and could pause to wonder why such things should be such a common feature of religion, I

93

might find they had something to tell me about entering what used to be called "the mysteries"? Perhaps they have something to do with entering the labyrinth of my mind and the nature of the realms of consciousness I might find there, where the laws of space and time and matter seem not to apply, or certainly to be different.

Do you not, now, believe that your right hand belongs to *you*—that it is yours? Do you not still answer the question, "To whom does that hand belong?" with the answer, "It belongs to me . . ." And, further, if you ask yourself the question, "Who do I mean when I say 'me'? Who is 'me'?" do you not answer, "I am". BUT are you *absolutely certain*, now, that the ego—the "me"—is also the *I*?

*

"When you enter the labyrinth, remember, you must find your own way back . . ."

*

Depending on how insistent the urge to find the truth is within me, so I will not be content to settle for inadequate, literal explanations. I will begin to penetrate deeper and I may find that, beyond the surface of religion as a discipline for mind and body, and beyond obedience and worship of the god-idea, there are realms of experience and understanding that I seldom dreamed existed.

For man is an extraordinary creature as far as the capacity of his mind is concerned. Beyond the question of his conduct in this world and the relative insignificance of his transitory ego are the realms of wider consciousness wherein lies his constant and fulfilling nature, his real "I".

Man—you and me—needs to consider the question of religion because within his human nature he is a *spiritual* being—one who can understand the almighty *spirit* ("spirit—the vital principle . . .") which enlivens him.

Of all the interests of man, religion—in the deep meaning of the word, being bound again to the real *I*—is the *only* one which can lead the way to lasting fulfilment.

*

What would be the point of man experiencing the deep questions of his innermost centre if there was no possibility of his being able to resolve them?

What would be the point of my being aware of the question "Who am I?" if there were not the possibility of discovering (removing the "covering" and, therefore, revealing?) who *I* am?

What can be the point of my being aware of my existence, if it is not possible to know why I exist, if it is not possible to know why I am aware that I am?

And what is the explanation for there being a knowledge that my body dies unless it be that that which knows it does not die?

*

Ultimately, if all was to be revealed to *me*, or if *I* discovered it, then I would be left standing face to face with one final question— or rather set of questions:

"What does this universe mean to me?" or/and *"What am I to this universe?"*

Eight

What does this universe mean to me? or What am I to this universe?

As the questions present themselves in my mind, the tendency is to reduce them to a manageable, recognizable size.

Because my mind cannot see beyond itself—any more than a shadow can see through the object that is creating it—it does not know the source of the questions. Not knowing the source, it believes itself to be the creator of the questions, and, believing thus, it cannot accept that it may be asking itself questions that it is incapable of answering.

Mind tries very hard to answer the questions. But, when it fails, its reaction is to drop them and turn its attention either to dreams, to imaginings or to more tangible subject matter—to things that it believes it already knows about.

If, however, the deep questions persist, if they will not be ignored, then one of two things usually seems to happen. The questions fuse the mind—rather like insufficient data can fuse, or confuse, a computer—causing the mind either to *break down*, or to *give up*.

*

Perhaps if I could see it, it would become clear that every mental disorder—however extreme—stems from mind having wrestled with some thought or idea which it was unable to process.

It is an interesting speculation—albeit only a speculation—that mental institutions, the world over, may be filled with people who came close to the centre of the labyrinth and then could not *remember* the way out again. Stuck there, near the centre, they suffer what the world calls a "mental breakdown", and all manner of therapies and treatments are attempted to bring them back to "normality". (The "norm" being how the *majority* behave, think, and conduct themselves outside the labyrinth). The "breakdown" is seen as the result of the patient having taken the wrong direction. Very rarely, if ever, is it considered that the patient may have taken the only direction for him—and therefore the appropriate direction?—but without sufficient food and equipment to continue the journey.

However, that is mere speculation and the "breakdown" remains one of the dire hazards of life today.

*

The second alternative—the mind "giving up"—we must all have experienced in one way or another.

I cannot remember someone's name. They have appeared before me, out of context, where I least expect to see them, and, although I know them well, their name entirely escapes me! What an agony of confusion the mind experiences. I know the name, but I cannot remember it. The name is on "the tip of my tongue", but I cannot bring it to mind.

What happens?

Eventually mind gives up the struggle, it dodges the issue, feigns a knowledge that it doesn't at that moment possess and avoids having to use the name.

Later in the day, when I am concerned with something far removed from the experience of not remembering the person's name, when mind has in fact "given up" the struggle, apparently out of the blue beyond . . . the name is remembered! It is not so amazing, for *I* had known it all the time. But what is it that stopped *me* remembering it when it was needed?

*

"Remember" is an interesting word in the English language—does it not mean precisely what it says? "Re", again; "member", parts, organs and particularly limbs; Re-member, re-limb, put together again—make it *whole*?

*

There is one other peculiarity in the way the mind works that I must look at, and that is the method it employs in order that it may function.

Mind appears to use a relative process—it thinks in dualities.

There is truth—because there is untruth.

There is happiness—because there is sadness.

There is light—because there is darkness.

There is high—because there is low, fat because there is thin, big and small, good and bad, right and wrong, young and old, beauty and ugliness—and so on, ad infinitum. The list is endless and covers every aspect of the world of mind.

But what mind, and the ego—*me*—who listens to mind, so often fails to notice is that these dualities are entirely dependent upon a third point standing between them—the *point of view*, the point from which the viewing takes place.

A flower towers above a tiny insect but is crushed under the foot of an elephant. Was *the flower* either high or low?

A piece of rotting meat is useless to a starving man, it will poison him. But the same piece of meat is vital food for the larvae of a fly or for the soil in which it is decomposing. Is the rotting meat poisonous, and therefore bad, or life-giving food, and therefore good?

This dualistic-thinking goes on wherever I look in the physical world, for all *things* are seen in relationship to *me*.

However, in the world of emotions, where feelings and sensations occur, it is not so easy to grasp.

I may pay lip service to the idea that "beauty is in the eye of the beholder" and that there can be no absolute beauty, but nevertheless, I have very definite ideas about what is beautiful and what is ugly and I make such judgements all the time.

As for *truth*, here again, I have very positive opinions. *Truth* is what I believe the truth to be. To say that the world is flat is ntruth, because I believe it to be round; but if I had lived at a ime when all people believed the world to be flat, and consequently I also held that belief, would I then have been untruthful to say that the world was flat?

Even here the duality depends upon the point of view—on *my* viewing.

It seems to me that there is sunrise and sunset. And yet I learn that the earth revolves round the sun. From the sun's point of view, it neither rises nor sets.

Sunrise and sunset are true from my relative viewpoint; but it is an illusion—in truth the sun shines all the time.

Perhaps there is only truth—and untruth is simply ignorance, the ignoring, or the not understanding, of truth?

*

The suggestion that there is only truth and that untruth is simply ignorance is a very far reaching concept.

If it is so, then does it not seem possible that *I* contain truth or, conversely, it contains *me*?

Clearly the entire conflict is in my mind.

Is it too much for me to suppose that if my mind were consciously to "give up", then the truth "I am" would enlighten my *whole* being?

*

It could be that my mind can never know the truth? But could it not also be that *to the degree that I recognize and relinquish the untruth, so may the truth reveal itself to me?*

Or am I flying too high and supposing too much?

*

As the journey into the labyrinth continues such seemingly outlandish notions form in the mind.

Are they dreams or imaginings? Are they even a sign of imminent "madness"? Possibly. But where do they come from, and why do they come?

For *mind* they represent a threat, because they do not belong to the rational world; worse, they seem to suggest that mind is wanting —that it is not equipped to deal with them, and that possibly it would be best if it did "give up".

But we cannot do without mind—how could we perform the simplest action, make the smallest communications or indeed continue to live, if mind was not constantly processing information and governing all our bodily functions?

Perhaps it is a case of allowing *mind* to get on with its work and at the same time disciplining it not to interfere where it doesn't and cannot, belong? A time for it to do its work, a time for it to be still?

*

The complexities multiply with every step that I seem to take, and often grave doubts arise as to whether I want to concern myself with the deep questions at all.

Once I begin to realize that the answers are not going to be easily obtained and that I may be embarking upon a life-time's work, then I am bound to ask:

Where do I go from here?

And

Do I want to go any further?

*

A friend, who is interested in words and who is committed to continuing the journey to the centre of the labyrinth, once observed that the word "question", in the English language, could perhaps in itself hold a vital clue, as it is made up of three words:

Quest I on.

It is as if the answer to: Where do I go from here? is simply— *Quest I on.* Keep questioning. Neither accept nor reject any answer until it is made *whole* in you—until, in fact, it is *re-membered*.

If *I* keep questioning, then the quest continues of itself.

Perhaps it is not a case of me becoming "holy"—just a case of ceasing to believe that I am not whole?

*

But do I *want* to go any further?

This can only be answered by each of us for "ourself", and will probably be answered differently from moment to moment.

If the quest is left entirely to the mind, then it is pretty certain that we will all give up sooner or later. No one will continue indefinitely in a state of bewilderment, not out of choice!

However, it is not only the head that is employed on this journey; it is not only the head that seeks peace.

The heart also is troubled by the deep questions, and the heart's experiences play an important role in encouraging us to continue into the labyrinth. It has been called "the longing of the heart".

*

The experience of *love* flowing from the heart is a mystery that is not easily spoken about. We have already discussed, in a previous chapter, the impossibility of expressing our emotions in physical terms—of describing the weight of our love or the height of our desire. However, if we are to pursue the religious question we must have some understanding of what we mean when we speak of love, what it seems to be, and what experiencing it does to *me*. For we will discover that it is the essential ingredient and power in *all* religious life.

*

The first *love* that any of us will have known will be in our infancy. It is the love for our parents or guardian and, on the face of it, it appears to flow in response to our being cared for, fed, protected and sustained. Usually there is a reciprocal love flowing back to us from the parent, and perhaps we are aware of this; we are "bathed in love".

As the physical body matures, the sex energy—that great powerhouse in the body—emerges and begins to play a dominant part in all our activities. Our growing awareness of the world about us, and the other people in that world, engrosses us. We select types that attract us, and this attraction stimulates the sexual desires in us. Certain people, we notice, arouse us physically—we are sexually aware of them. We find that we desire the attention and company of one particular person because we admire that person and because with that person we feel stimulated, and freed from the preoccupations of the mind—the person can take *me* out of myself. Soon we are saying that we are "in love" with that person.

But who is "in love"? And what is this state, or place, that we refer to as "love" and into which we feel we have entered?

As my sexual attraction matures I find that I wish to possess the other person. I want to be part of that person, to merge—body with body, mind with mind—to become, in fact, *one* with that person.

The sexual act is a strong, potent experience with overwhelming repercussions upon body and upon mind. If the orgasm, the climax of mutual surrender, is reached, the two bodies and the two minds, for a moment, are joined in the one experience. In that moment there is *union*, *oneness*, the *two* have become *one*. Me, the ego, sacrifices its separate identity.

Throughout the history and literature of the world, poets speak of this moment as the highest experience attainable by man.

It does seem to have the capacity for throwing mind into the wildest confusion!

We speak about being "head over heels in love"!

The procreation of the species takes place in the name of this sexual love; men have fought duels and murdered in its name; whole nations have gone to war for it; houses are built, food is grown and money is obtained for the sake of such love.

But what *is* it?

Certainly it seems to have little to do with the methodical working out of explanations that mind relies upon. In fact it seems that it can dominate mind—it can change or obliterate mind in a moment.

When I am in love, nothing else seems to matter. I am entirely consumed by it. My every action and thought is directed towards the object of my desire. I will go through hell and high water simply to be by my beloved's side. I will not even care for my own well-being, so obsessed am I with my desire.

But what that desire *is* it is hard to say. What is it that I expect from the other person? Why should another person do this to me? Is the other person doing it, or is what is happening entirely *my* doing?

Usually what happens is that the first, careless, out-going experience of love becomes dominated by the sexual urge—pleasure, power, possession.

So strong is this urge that we lose sight of the person as a *whole*, and seek only the body. We seek to possess the body or to be possessed by it. Mind recovers from the initial shock and gets to work. The person has a mind—it also can be possessed or can possess. My mind tries to change your mind—see it *my* way, ego says, or, teach me to see it *your* way.

The result . . . chaos? Not always. For what we have been discussing is *sexual* attraction.

Love, with which we started is altogether more subtle.

If we return to that first simple example of the infant bathed in the protective love of its parent or guardian, we are perhaps getting closer to that essential love-experience that is at the centre of all human relationship—for, why is it that *I* desire to relate to someone, if it is not that *I* desire not to be separate, to be in union, to be *one*?

Such a feeling of love, when it stirs in us, is like a warm current flowing from the heart, enveloping the body, albeit for brief moments, in the secure sense of well-being and wholeness. Once we have had such an experience—and we are suggesting that we *all* have had it in our infancy—it is never forgotten and is constantly looked for.

It comes when least expected, when least looked for. The beauty of nature, of a flower or an animal or a still, shining lake, can bring it to us. The smile of recognition, the touch of a loved one, a piece of music, a great work of art or a simple, kindly gesture of response . . . the ways that the love in us may be released are legion and often unexpected. There even are times when love flows in our bodies for no apparent reason. Then, suddenly, there is a moment of gentle warmth, and a sense of being complete. You want for nothing, there is no desire to claim anything, it is wonderfully sufficient simply to be alive.

If this has been experienced—then does it not feel very right, peculiarly familiar? Almost as if it were our natural and fulfilled state?

We speak of "falling in love". Is it not as if the state of love is ever present and that sometimes, as if by chance, we "fall" into it?

But it is not my permanent state. What is it, I wonder, that separates *me* from it most of the time?

*

In all religious traditions this pure love experience plays an essential role.

Volumes of scriptures speak of the love of the deity and the devout worshipper will, in turn, speak of his or her love for the deity.

But what is it that they are loving, and what is it that they believe is loving them?

How may I love something or somebody that I know precious little about?

How may I experience the love of something or somebody that I have not seen, or touched, or *communicated* with. ("Communion" —to come into union.) How can there be love without an object of union?

So crucial is this paradox that in many religious traditions men have grown to love the exponent of the particular religious tradition in the place of the mysterious deity that he is speaking about. The Christ, the Buddha, the prophet Mohammed become the object of deep devotion and love for the followers of that particular tradition. (And the priest, the rabbi, the bhikku, in his turn can enjoy the love and the respect of his congregation.)

Why is it so important for them to have someone to love?

Is it because—not knowing who *I* am—I require an outward manifestation to love in the place of *me*?

I cannot love *me* because *me* varies and disappoints and some- times is far from lovable. Not being able in all sincerity to love *me*, but experiencing nevertheless the strong, vital urge to *love* within *me*—I must seek outside myself for a love-object.

And in that moment when love is fulfilled, when "I am in love" do I not, in loving the other person, experience that love flowing throughout myself?

And is it not only then that I feel whole?

I may not know who I am—but I am full of love; I love who I am.

In that moment, ego is transcended. *I* am literally above ego, *I* contain every facet of *me*—*I am* whole *in* love.

The union that *I* have been seeking—that union between the ego and I—has been realized.

*

What has all this got to do with our journey through the labyrinth and, more particularly, with the question of religion?

Is it possible that to be *in* love, in the religious sense—to be *in* the deity's love—as a permanent state, might be the utter holiness of being dead to myself but in total communion with the oneness of everything?

*

During the "dark ages" a great deal of time and effort was spent in attempting to turn dross into gold.

This science or art was called "alchemy".

Here, very roughly, is the recipe that was employed:

First, take your base metal and grind it down until it is dust.

Then take a quantity of quick-silver (mercury) and mix it with the base metal.

Then find a way to hold the quick-silver and make it still and motionless.

Holding the still mixture over a flame—heat it.

Then introduce a single particle of pure gold.

And, in time, the base metal mixture will be united with the particle of gold and the whole will become gold.

I know of no record that claims that this recipe actually worked —if it had, there would have been an inflationary situation and very soon gold would have become worthless, and therefore not worth making!

So what were the alchemists talking about?

Are we looking at a perfect *simile* for quite another process?
The base metal—the ego; grind it down under pressure.
Quick silver—the mind; find a way to make it still and quiet.
The flame—the heart.
The heat of the flame—*love*, suffusing the body and the mind.
The particle of gold—truth, higher knowledge, "wisdom".
Perhaps . . .

*

If we are now living in a "dark age", then the question of religion becomes the only question *I* desire to pursue, because it is in the religious traditions that the knowledge that we require—the particle of gold—may possibly have been preserved.

However, man is a busy animal, and he has put centuries of his own interpretation upon what is contained in the writings and the beliefs of the traditions. If I am to find the gold in them I must search with painstaking precision. I must trust that I will recognize what I am looking for when it appears.

If, within a certain tradition, I learn many wonders and realize many mysteries all well and good—but, if I still cannot answer the questions within myself—if I still cannot answer "Who am I?" —then I will know that I am still not at the centre of the labyrinth, that I still haven't finished the quest.

For, *I* will not be wholly fulfilled until I know *I am*.

And, in the final analysis, is that not precisely what each of us is looking for—complete fulfilment in this life and a clear understanding of what death means?

Man is indeed a wonderful creation, for he has the capacity to enter upon this quest; and, if the capacity to search is there—is it too much to suppose that the possibility of finding is also there, for each and every one of us? Then would man discover his spirit and be with the gods?

*

"*I have hidden it where man will never think of looking for it.
I have hidden it within Man himself.*"

*

In this book an attempt has been made to look at the predicament that the ego experiences while it is cut off from the centre of the labyrinth, when it is lost in a maze of belief and assumption.

An attempt has also been made to explore the possible way that anyone requiring the answers to the deep questions may proceed—by understanding, listening to, and penetrating the questions themselves.

If we proceed from here to examine the religious traditions that have been handed down through the centuries, perhaps we will not now be bewildered by their quaint and mysterious language. We will be looking to see what they have to say about such things as discipline and right conduct of mind and body, about faith, love, relationships, holiness, immortality and so on—not as theoretical concepts that someone once spoke about years ago but how they may apply to my experience of myself and the world, here and now.

*

Do we have to bother with the questions at all? It depends whether I am content to be the victim of all the circumstances which assail me. If I am not, then I have to examine the beliefs, assumptions, attitudes and opinions that I hold. To the extent that I discard that which I find unreasonable, so my behaviour will change, becoming more directed and consistent. My ideas as to what I want to be and do will be modified and there will be confidence in my motives.

Basically, it is a choice between living a life of virtually total, purposeless, self-indulgence or discovering a purpose for my existence.

*

This is only a book that you have read. It has been written by two people—although throughout the book the two people have often spoken in the singular; "we" have spoken as "I". This is not a deception, for what we have explored has been a shared exploration, what has been seen has been a shared discovery.

During the book we have suggested the device of pausing—

giving the mind a rest. This seems to us to be essential, because once mind starts to tire it loses interest—and once it loses interest, it doesn't want to pursue the enquiry any further. It is interesting to note that most of the religious traditions also use devices for stilling the mind—meditation, contemplation, prayer, chanting and so on. But without the discipline and instructions of a particular tradition these activities—or non-activities?—are not easy to do. All that is needed is—to pause—to stop the mind, for a moment, in its tracks . . .

It is what the oldest and wisest of the gods said to man in our opening story:

"Nothing is ever found by rushing round in a circle. Be still. Find ways to become still . . .

"Be still, listen, your Spirit is asking for you".

For here is the strangest quality of the deep questions that have concerned us. If we listen to one of them—really listen . . .

"Who am I?"

. . . and we determinedly pull our attention away from the many answers that thinking mind is offering and focus again on the question . . .

"Who am I?"

. . . and again . . .

"Who am I?"

. . . and yet again . . .

"Who am I?"

. . . and if we devote a life-time to listening to the question; then it is possible that the very question itself may reveal the answers that head and heart have ever craved.

*

Not those fundamental, fact-answers of the world.

One plus One equals two. It is lawful, it can be seen to be so. But—what is the original *one*—and how can there be two *ones*, for that first step in addition?

It is the mystery of all creation.

What was there before the *one*?

Where did the *one* come from?

*

"*Who am I?*"
For the deepest questions there can only be the deepest answers.
And, for the final question?
Does *Truth* require an answer?

*

Is the god-idea man-invented—or is God the Self-evident Total
Reality revealed when all illusion is discarded?

*

The search may take us through all the great religious traditions
of the world—but it must also of necessity take each of us through
ourselves, through the labyrinth of mind to the very centre of our
being.

The devout seeker of the truth, when he approached the sanctuary
of Apollo at Delphi in ancient Greece saw, cut into the stones of
the temple in which the oracle resided, two sentences. They were
injunctions—guides for the quest.

The first referred to the religious disciplines of mind and body
which regulate our behaviour in this world:

"*Nothing in excess*"

The second referred to the search within each of us—for the
spirit, the truth—what you will. It was simple and direct:

"*Know thyself*"

The oracle at Delphi has been silent for many centuries—and
Apollo is no longer considered a deity. But the message of Delphi
lingers still in the minds of men.

Who am I? *The* question of religion.
KNOW THYSELF